Unquestionably Free

by LaKesha L. Williams

Foreword by Dr. Nathan Mizzell, bestselling author of
The Fight of My Life

Afterword by Dr. Tiajuana Smith Pittman, bestselling author
of *Uniquely Flawed*

Copyright © 2023 by The VTF Group LLC | The VTF Publishing House

All Scripture quotations are AMP unless otherwise indicated and are public domain courtesy of Bible Gateway: www.biblegateway.com

All Rights Reserved. No part of this publication may be reproduced, stored in a retrieval system, or transmitted in any form or by any means, electronic, mechanical, photocopying or otherwise, without the prior written permission of the copyright owner.

Paperback ISBN: 979-8-9869160-2-6
Hardback ISBN: 979-8-9869160-3-3
eBook ISBN: 979-8-9869160-4-0

Cover Design by LaKesha L. Williams (www.coachkesha.com)
Editing & Typesetting by Latricia C. Bailey (www.consultlatricia.com)
Published by The VTF Group LLC, Waldorf MD 20603

COACHING | PUBLISHING | CONSULTING

www.TheVTFGroup.com
For information about special discounts for bulk orders please contact:
The VTF Group LLC | The VTF Publishing House | The Vision to Fruition Publishing House
at: info@thevtfgroup.com

ALL RIGHTS RESERVED
PRINTED IN THE USA

Dedication

Written in Loving Memory of:

My grandmother, Maggie L. McNeill, who raised my mother, Doris M. Williams, to be a woman of God who raised me to be the woman of God that I am today!
Rest, until we meet again.
1916 - 1994

My brother in Christ, Rev. Anthony McCollum, the first official recipient of a Born Overcomers wristband, which he wore until the day God chose to call him home. Your presence and encouragement are dearly missed.
Rest, until we meet again.
1963 – 2015

Table of Contents

Opening...

Acknowledgements 2
Foreword 3
Preface 5
Introduction 25
Prologue 45

Overcoming...

Chapter 1 - Negative Thinking 51
Chapter 2 - Rape & Molestation 79
Chapter 3 – Lust 117
Chapter 4 – Impurity 175
Chapter 5 – Sickness 207
Chapter 6 – Ungratefulness 233
Chapter 7 – Shame 247
Chapter 8 – Free Indeed 269
Chapter 9 – Unquestionably Free 275

Closing...

Final Thoughts 293
Afterword 295
About the Author 301
About the Publisher 305

Acknowledgements

Without You, none of this would be. Without You, there would be no me. I praise You. I worship You. I honor You. I love You. I thank You God!

To my loving mom, Doris M. Williams, my superhero dad, Cleo R. Williams Jr., my amazing siblings, my awesome extended family, and my dope church family. Thank You for your continual, consistent love and support!

To my beautiful friend, Latricia, my wonderful friend, Vanessa, my covenant sister, Chris, and one of my biggest supporters, literally since day one, Darlene. Thank You for being the tribe I needed!

Foreword

Unquestionably Free by LaKesha L. Williams is one of the most captivating and skillfully written Kingdom books of our age. The Bible speaks of the importance of testifying of that which you have seen; that which you have heard; that which you have lived; and that which you have overcome. Having personally walked with LaKesha for some time, I can say without a doubt that she represents the epitome of a spiritual visionary, teacher, life coach, and friend. However, most of all she has proven herself to be an overcomer by the Blood of the Lamb and the word of her testimony.

While life offers many spectators, speculators, and sabotagers, rarely are we blessed to encounter spiritual surgeons anointed by God to be the pen in the hand of the ready writer serving as God-ordained compasses. They lead to the fresh pastures of overcoming life's most challenging tests, trials, and tribulations. LaKesha is one who has traveled down some of the darkest, destitute, desperate, disparaging, debilitating, and depressing paths of destruction and navigated through the valley of the shadow of death only to emerge as a true overcomer.

In her book ***Unquestionably Free***, LaKesha meticulously details her personal struggles with spirits of negative thinking, rape, lust, conformity, sickness, ungratefulness, and shame. Yet, the Lord uses her to remind us all that such battles are never between flesh and blood, but against principalities, powers, rulers of the darkness of the world, and spiritual wickedness in high places. Only with the help of the Lord are any of us empowered to overcome such challenges in life.

LaKesha pours out of her personal pain to preach and teach the grace gifts of salvation, deliverance, healing, wholeness, and true freedom through the lens of the Gospel of Jesus Christ. From fighting for her personal life to fighting for the souls of others, her timely, relevant, and resolute testimony serves to inspire and guide in the crucible of these pages, stimulating the spirit of her readers to awaken and choose to overcome any and every adversity they may ever face.

Congratulations on a job well done! May GOD continue to bless you and everyone who will read, subscribe to, share, and apply the principles of overcoming adversity outlined in this book!

God's Richest Blessings, Dr. Nathaniel Mizzell
The Fight of My Life: The Breaking and Making of a Leader
www.TheFightofMyLife.com

Preface

I am honored that you are reading this book right now. I am even more honored that you have made the choice to take this journey with me. This book is an enhanced and updated edition of Born Overcomers which was first released in July of 2014. I just wanted to take a moment to talk about how the first book and the Born Overcomers movement came to be. I had been preparing to write a book my entire life and didn't know it until early 2014. What you are reading is my 20th publication, but there would be no 20th without a 1st.

Back in 2014, I was thinking over my life and recalling all I have been through. As I thought back, I realized my past experiences would be an interesting book to read, but I had no clue how to write a book or how to start. So instead of writing a book I started a blog. I built a very small following, but I still felt I should write a book. Around this same time, I began seeing a therapist to deal with the traumas of my past. These therapy sessions helped me realize a lot about myself, all God had done in my life and all God wanted to do through my life. With the encouragement of my therapist and these discoveries, I was able to begin writing.

I had big plans in the beginning, the first title of the book was *The Promise*. I planned on guiding readers through four steps: 1) pain, 2) process, 3) purpose, and 4) promise. These four steps would lead the reader to discover their purpose in life and accept the promise and call of God on their life. I wrote one full chapter and was stuck for about six months. Nothing more was coming for me to write. I was so frustrated because I knew God called me to write a book, and I didn't know why I couldn't write.

I had already begun sharing my testimony on social media and via the blog, so why was it so hard to write? I mean I was writing my testimony and I was there for the whole thing, so why the writer's block? Little did I know God had other plans for how this book was going to come to fruition and all that would be attached to the book.

January 31, 2014, my employment status changed. God then revealed there was so much more He wanted me to do in this life than just work as an IT Service Desk Supervisor. It was then I really began seeking Him for what my next steps were. Between February and May of 2014, God was continually revealing things to me about how He wanted me to share my testimony and be an encouragement to His people.

Monday June 2, 2014, I was meeting with a business coach and although we were getting to know each other and talking about our businesses, she really inspired me to finish what I had started months ago. That day a fire was ignited. That same day after I met with her, I went to the library to spend some time with God, to see how He wanted me to move forward. I booked a quiet room at the library from 1:00 pm to 4:00 pm. I sat down and prayed for God to download His vision. It was that day, Monday June 2, 2014, God gave me the idea for the 1st book.

I asked God, "What is it You want Your people to take away from this book?" God revealed, all I have witnessed, experienced and been through could be used as tools to encourage others to overcome. The foundation of my testimony and the Born Overcomers Movement is Revelation 12:11, which says, *¹¹And they overcame and conquered him because of the Blood of the Lamb and because of the word of their testimony, for they did not love their life and renounce their faith even when faced with death.*

Revelation 12:11 gives Christians three effective spiritual strategies to use to overcome Satan's attacks upon our lives.

1. *And they overcame and conquered him because of the blood of the Lamb…*
Over 2000 years ago Jesus died on The Cross for our sins and sicknesses. His Blood was shed for our sins. The Lamb in this Scripture refers to Jesus Christ our Lord and Savior. Because

God sent His only Begotten Son Jesus to be the ultimate sacrifice for our sins, we are redeemed, victorious, and overcomers. We needed this to happen to be overcomers. The shed Blood of Jesus provides cleansing of our sins and protection against the attacks of the enemy.

2. *...and because of the word of their testimony...*
We all have probably heard it once said, "You can't have a testimony, without first having a test!" To take that even further, we cannot have a testimony without the Word.

John 1:1 talks about the deity of Jesus Christ, it says, *In the beginning [before all-time] was the Word (Christ), and the Word was with God, and the Word was God Himself.* What Jesus taught and what He did are inseparably tied to who He is. In this passage of Scripture, John shows Jesus as fully human and fully God. Although Jesus took upon Himself full humanity and lived as a man, He never ceased to be the eternal God who has always existed, the Creator and Sustainer of all things, and the source of eternal life. This is the truth about Jesus, and the foundation of all truth. If we cannot or do not believe this basic truth, we will not have enough faith to entrust our eternal destiny to Him. That is why John wrote this Gospel—to build faith and confidence in Jesus Christ so that we may believe that He truly was and is the Son of God.

To overcome we must first accept Jesus Christ as our Lord and Savior. A requirement of successfully overcoming is having a relationship with the Ultimate Overcomer! In addition to accepting Christ, to activate this innate characteristic of overcoming the enemy, we must read the Word and apply the Word daily, which results in us developing a testimony as we move from glory to glory and begin to walk in freedom.

****

Do you ever think that because you aren't good enough for God, He will not save you? Do you ever feel as if salvation is for everyone else but you? If God gave His Son for you, He isn't going to hold back the gift of salvation! If Christ gave His life for you, He isn't going to turn around and condemn you! He will not withhold anything you need to live for Him.

Let's talk about how to accept Jesus Christ as your Lord and Savior. If you do not know Christ this is where you can begin a relationship with Him by praying the prayer of salvation!

Confessing Our Sin
When we pray the prayer of salvation, we admit that we've sinned. As the Bible says of everyone in Romans 3:22-25, save Christ alone: *²²This righteousness of God comes through faith in Jesus Christ for all those [Jew or Gentile] who believe [and trust in Him and acknowledge Him as God's Son]. There is no*

distinction, ²³since all have sinned and continually fall short of the glory of God, ²⁴and are being justified [declared free of the guilt of sin, made acceptable to God, and granted eternal life] as a gift by His [precious, undeserved] grace, through the redemption [the payment for our sin] which is [provided] in Christ Jesus, ²⁵whom God displayed publicly [before the eyes of the world] as a [life-giving] sacrifice of atonement and reconciliation (propitiation) by His blood [to be received] through faith. This was to demonstrate His righteousness [which demands punishment for sin], because in His forbearance [His deliberate restraint] He passed over the sins previously committed [before Jesus' crucifixion]."

Justified means to be declared not guilty. When a judge in a court of law declares the defendant not guilty, all charges are removed from his record. Legally, it is as if the person had never been accused. When God forgives our sins, our record is wiped clean. From His perspective, it is as though we never sinned.

Redemption refers to Christ setting sinners free from slavery and bondage to sin. In Old Testament times, a person's debts could result in his being sold as a slave. The next of kin could redeem him—buy his freedom. Christ bought our freedom, and the price was His life.

Christ is our propitiation (atonement or reparation for a wrong or injury). In other words, He died in our place, for our sins. God is justifiably angry at sinners. They have rebelled against Him and cut themselves off from His life-giving power. But God declares Christ's death to be the right, designated sacrifice for our sin. Christ then stands in our place, having paid the penalty of death for our sin, and He completely satisfies God's demands. His sacrifice brings pardon, deliverance, and freedom.

What happened to people who lived before Christ came and died for sin? If God condemned them, was He being unfair? If He saved them, was Christ's sacrifice unnecessary? Paul shows that God forgave all human sin at the Cross of Jesus. Old Testament believers looked forward in faith to Christ's coming and were saved, even though they did not know Jesus' name or the details of His earthly life. Unlike Old Testament believers, you know about the God who loved the world so much that He gave His own Son. Have you put your trust in Him?

After all this bad news about our sinfulness and God's condemnation, Paul gives the wonderful news. There is a way to be declared not guilty—by trusting Jesus Christ to take away our sins. Trusting means putting our confidence in Christ to forgive our sins, to make us right with God, and to empower us to live the way He taught us. God's solution is available to us regardless of our background or past behavior.

Some sins seem bigger than others because their obvious consequences are more serious. Murder, for example, seems to us to be worse than hatred, and adultery seems worse than lust. All sins make us sinners, and all sin cuts us off from our Holy God. All sin, therefore, leads to death because it disqualifies us from living with God, regardless of how great or small it seems. Don't minimize "little" sins or overrate "big" sins. They all separate us from God, but they all can be forgiven.

To sin is simply to fall short of the mark, like an arrow that does not quite hit the bullseye. The glory of God, that we fall short of is found only in Jesus Christ. Second Corinthians 4:6 says, *⁶For God, who said, "Let light shine out of darkness," is the One who has shone in our hearts to give us the Light of the knowledge of the glory and majesty of God [clearly revealed] in the face of Christ.*

The prayer of salvation, then, recognizes that Jesus Christ is the only human who ever lived without sin. Second Corinthians 5:21 says, *²¹He made Christ who knew no sin to [judicially] be sin on our behalf, so that in Him we would become the righteousness of God [that is, we would be made acceptable to Him and placed in a right relationship with Him by His gracious lovingkindness]*. When we trust in Christ, we make an exchange—our sin for His righteousness. Our sin was poured into Christ at His crucifixion. His righteousness is poured into us at our conversion. This is what Christians mean by Christ's atonement for sin. In the world, bartering works only when two people exchange goods of relatively equal value. But God offers to trade His righteousness for our sin—something of immeasurable worth for something completely worthless. How grateful we should be for His kindness to us.

Professing Faith in Christ as your Savior and Lord
With Christ as our standard of perfection, we're now acknowledging faith in Him as God, agreeing with the Apostle John in John 1:2-3, where it says, *²He was [continually existing] in the beginning [co-eternally] with God. ³All things were made and came into existence through Him; and without Him not even one thing was made that has come into being.* When God created, He made something out of nothing. Since we are created beings, we have no basis for pride. Remember that you exist only because God made you, and you have special gifts only because God gave them to you. With God you are something valuable and unique; apart from God you are nothing, and if you try to live without Him, you will be abandoning the purpose for which you were made.

God could only accept a perfect, sinless sacrifice, and since He knew that we could not possibly accomplish that, He sent

His Son to die for us and pay the eternal price. John 3:16 says, *¹⁶For God so [greatly] loved and dearly prized the world, that He [even] gave His [One and] only begotten Son, so that whoever believes and trusts in Him [as Savior] shall not perish but have eternal life.*

Say It Aloud & Mean It Now!
Do you agree with everything you have read so far? If so, don't wait a moment longer to start your new life in Jesus Christ. Remember, this prayer is not a magical formula. You are simply expressing your heart to God. Pray this with me:

Father, I know that I have broken Your laws and my sins have separated me from You. I am truly sorry, and now I want to turn away from my past sinful life, toward You. Please forgive me and help me avoid sinning again. I believe that Your Son, Jesus Christ died for my sins, was resurrected from the dead, is alive, and hears my prayer. I invite Jesus to become the Lord of my life, to rule and reign in my heart from this day forward. Please send your Holy Spirit to help me obey You, and to do Your will for the rest of my life. In Jesus' name, I pray, Amen.

I've Prayed; Now What?
If you've prayed this prayer of salvation with true conviction and heart, you are now a follower of Jesus. This is a fact, whether you feel any different or not. Religious systems may have led you to believe that you should feel something—a

warm glow, a tingle, or some other mystical feeling. The fact is, you may, or you may not. If you have prayed the prayer of salvation and meant it, you are now a follower of Jesus. The Bible tells us in Romans 10:9, that your eternal salvation is secure, *9...because if you acknowledge and confess with your mouth that Jesus is Lord [recognizing His power, authority, and majesty as God], and believe in your heart that God raised Him from the dead, you will be saved.*

Welcome to the family of God! I encourage you now to find a local church where you can be baptized and grow in the knowledge of God through His Word, the Bible.

Now back to the third and last strategy to use to overcome Satan's attacks upon our lives.

****

3. *...for they did not love their life and renounce their faith even when faced with death.*
The last strategy is total surrender. Totally surrendering to God means that even if called to do so—we would die as a martyr for one's faith in Jesus Christ.

These three strategies; using the Blood of the Lamb, the Word of our testimony and total surrender activate the Spirit within us to overcome the attacks of the enemy and walk in total freedom. The critical blow to Satan came when the Lamb, Jesus Christ, shed His Blood for our lives. The victory is won by sacrifice—Christ's death in our place to pay the penalty for our sin, and the sacrifices we make because of our faith in Him. As we face the battle with Satan, we should not fear it or try to escape from it, but we should loyally serve Christ, who alone brings victory.

Romans 8:37 says, *³⁵Who shall ever separate us from the love of Christ? Will tribulation, distress, or persecution, or famine, or nakedness, or danger, or sword? ³⁶Just as it is written and forever remains written, "FOR YOUR SAKE WE ARE PUT TO DEATH ALL DAY LONG; WE ARE REGARDED AS SHEEP FOR THE SLAUGHTER." ³⁷Yet in all these things we are more than conquerors and gain an overwhelming victory through Him who loved us [so much that He died for us].*

These verses hold one of the most comforting promises in all Scripture. Believers have always had to face hardships in many forms: persecution, illness, imprisonment, even death. These could cause them to fear that they have been abandoned by Christ. But Paul exclaims that it is *impossible* to be separated from Christ. His death for us is proof of His unconquerable love. Nothing can stop Christ's constant presence with us. God tells us how great His love is so that we will feel totally secure in Him. If we believe these overwhelming assurances, we will not be afraid.

I felt it was important to break these strategies down because Revelation 12:11 gives me the permission and the authority to boldly share my testimony. So, as we flashback to Monday June 2, as I sat in that library quiet room, I began to search and cross reference Scriptures that were attached to Revelation 12:11, searching for a different perspective and possibly a different title because *The Promise* was not it.

Next on my search for a title, I came up with *We Shall Overcome* but that just didn't resonate. I continued searching. The next title that came was *The Blood of the Lamb*, but that one did not fit either. I wasn't having an *AHA, that's it!* moment when I thought of these titles. So, I continued searching and I came across Psalm 139:16 (NLT) which says, *¹⁶You saw me before I was born. Every day of my life was recorded in Your book. Every moment was laid out before a single day had passed.*

These three truths can be gleaned from Psalm 139:16:

1. *You saw me before I was born.*
Before you were born God saw you, He knew you and He knew who and what you would become. Jeremiah 1:5, says, *¹Before I formed you in the womb, I knew you [and approved of you as My chosen instrument], And before you were born, I consecrated you [to Myself as My own]; I have appointed you as a prophet to the nations.* God knew you, as He knew Jeremiah, long before

you were born or even conceived. He thought about you and planned for you. When you feel discouraged or inadequate, remember that God has always thought of you as valuable and that He has a purpose in mind for you.

Jeremiah was "appointed" by God as a "prophet to the nations" God has a purpose for each Christian, but some people are appointed by God for specific kinds of work. Samson (see Judges 13:3-5), David (see 1 Samuel 16:12-13), John the Baptist (see Luke 1:13-17), and Paul (see Galatians 1:15-16) were also called to do jobs for God. Whatever work you do should be done for the glory of God. If God has not given you a specific call or assignment, then seek to fulfill the mission common to all believers—to love, obey and serve God—until His guidance becomes clearer.

The New International Translation of this Scripture reads, *¹Before I formed you in the womb I knew you, before you were born, I set you apart; I appointed you as a prophet to the nations.* If you research the words *set apart,* you will find they are connected to the word holiness. According to Merriam Webster, the word holiness is a noun that means *state or character of being holy.* Holy is also an adjective that means *belonging to, derived from, or associated with a divine power* and *set apart to the service of God.* In other words, that which is holy belongs to God. It is sanctified, meaning *set apart for a holy use or purpose.*

Before you were born God deemed you as holy, He set you apart for His holy use and purpose. God created you and I with a purpose, you did not enter this world just because your parents hooked up; your introduction to this world was predesigned by God Himself. God did not bring you into this world just to suffer and experience hardships.

In the last part of Jeremiah 1:5, in God's message to Jeremiah, He lets him know exactly what his purpose is, it says, *I appointed you as a Prophet to the nations.* Before Jeremiah was born and even before the foundation of this Earth, God knew him, God had set him apart and God had appointed him, and so it is with you and me.

2. *Every day of my life was recorded in Your book.*
Every single day, hour, minute and second, God recorded about you before you ever came to be, before the Earth ever came to be! This sentence I believe is the most important of the three sentences and how fitting for it to be sandwiched in the middle like an Oreo (we all know the cream is the best part). Again, it says, every day of your life was recorded in God's book! So that tells me that if every day was recorded, then He already knew what you would go through and what you would experience right? Hence the very reason you're a Born Overcomer! He already knew and He gave you everything you needed from the very beginning to overcome everything that would come your way in this life. I want you

to memorize this Scripture and when something happens, or when things aren't going your way, I want you to say this out loud and remember everything that happens is a part of God's plan because: *Every day of your life was recorded in His book!*

3. *Every moment was laid out before a single day had passed.*
Guess what, this very moment; holding this book in your hands or reading it on your device; was laid out before a single day had passed. How freeing is it to know that despite what your current circumstances are God allowed it because He knew you could handle it. He knew it would only make you stronger, enhance your testimony and enable you to help others overcome!

Psalm 139:16 led me to begin thinking over my life and all I had been through. I kept reading this Scripture repeatedly, wondering why I was stuck here, then it dawned on me: *If God knew me before I was born, then He knew all I'd endure, which means He equipped me to overcome before my life even started.* This could only mean I was born to overcome. This was my *AHA, that's it!* moment, I literally felt like I had just won a trillion dollars because I'd just discovered the title of the first book: *Born Overcomers*!

From that moment God began revealing things to me about the first book and how He wanted me to move forward. He showed me Born Overcomers was going to be more than just a book. It was still Monday June 2, 2014.

Tuesday June 3, 2014, I was sharing how God gave me the title of the book with someone; she mentioned something about a Facebook group. That night I created a Facebook group. Wednesday June 4, 2014, I was sharing with someone else how God gave me the book title and she mentioned something about a conference, that same day I began looking for venues for the 1st Annual Born Overcomers Conference. I also developed a website and filed to become a 501(c)3 nonprofit organization with the State of Maryland. By the end of the week the Facebook group had grown to more than 1,000 members, I had a 12-member team on board to help me and we had decided on a location in Lanham Maryland to hold the first conference.

At the time of this writing, it is October 2022, and it has been eight years, since God birth Born Overcomers Inc. Since then, I have written ten books and co-authored six anthologies including one with actress and comedian Kim Coles. God has allowed Born Overcomers Inc. to become an internationally recognized non-profit organization that holds annual conferences, quarterly testimony parties and provides outreach in the community. From the publication of my first book, an international Hybrid Publishing House was created and as a result God has birth more than 110 authors through

The Vision to Fruition Publishing House, which is a subsidiary of The VTF Group LLC. The Glory is His alone, because only God could have orchestrated all that has come to fruition since Monday June 4, 2014.

As we endured the pandemic, I was seeking God about what was next, and He downloaded the book you hold in your hands today. The first few books were an introduction to overcoming, this book is a guide to freedom inspired by true events. This book is only a continuation of what was started all those years ago. I am grateful to God for using me to birth this ministry and this new book. I pray that you are encouraged by what you read in this book. The purpose of this book is to show you what freedom looks like and how to maintain it on the other side of overcoming.

After reading this book, I pray you will feel:

1. Inspired to overcome.
2. Equipped to keep the freedom found in overcoming.
3. Encouraged to never go back to the thing that had you bound.
4. Drawn to grow in deeper intimacy with God, because it's there you will find the freedom you have been looking for.

Seek God as you read, ask Him to reveal areas in your life where you want to overcome and experience freedom. Search and memorize Scriptures related to those areas and earnestly seek to overcome them. Remember there is freedom on the other side of overcoming.

Introduction

I am a summation of everything I have experienced in my 40 years of life. Every hurt, pain, joy, happy moment, worry, and doubt have all been orchestrated by God. Before I was born, God had written my story. He knew—my purpose, my pain, what I would be like, who I would be, what I would like and dislike, and even who my family, friends, and associates would be. He knew my purpose and He knew through His Son Jesus; I would be equipped to overcome this world and live free from the bondage of sin.

John 16:33 says, *[33]I have told you these things, so that in Me you may have [perfect] peace. In the world you have tribulation and distress and suffering, but be courageous [be confident, be undaunted, be filled with joy]; I have overcome the world." [My conquest is accomplished, My victory abiding.]*

With these words Jesus told His disciples to take courage. Despite the inevitable struggles they would face, they would not be alone. Jesus does not abandon us to our struggles either. If we remember that the ultimate victory has already been won, we can claim the peace of Christ in the most troublesome times.

You were created on purpose. You are not an accident or a mistake. Rather, you are fearfully and wonderfully made. You are unconditionally loved by God. Not only were you created on purpose, but you also have a purpose for your life that God is working for your good. You are valuable to God. He sees so much value in you that He gave His only Son, Jesus, to save you. You have worth and a purpose!

Merriam Webster defines the word purpose as the reason for which something exists or is done, made or used. God created you on purpose, with a purpose, for a purpose. God created you for a reason. We exist because God wants us to, God needs us to fulfill His purposes in the earth. Genesis 1:31 says, *"God saw everything that He had made, and behold, it was very good, and He validated it completely."* Guess who was a part of this *very good* creation? If you said, *I am!* You're correct!!

I want to bring attention to the word *validated*. According to Merriam-Webster, the word validate means to recognize, establish, or illustrate worthiness or legitimacy of. God *completely* recognized, established, and illustrated the worthiness and legitimacy of your existence from the foundation of the world.

Genesis 1:31 tells us God saw that all He had created was excellent in every way. You are a part of God's creation, and He is pleased with how He made you. If at times you feel worthless or of little value, remember that God made you for a good reason. You are valuable to Him. Now I know, for many, this is a hard concept to grasp with all we experience in our lives. And honestly, I didn't always believe I was valuable to Him myself. But God relentlessly pursues those whom He has called and chosen.

How do you determine the value of something? An object's value is determined by the price someone is willing to pay for the item. Jesus paid a price for you. When we realize the price Jesus paid for our freedom, we can live free from bondage. Matthew 20:28 says, *²⁸...just as the Son of Man did not come to be served, but to serve, and to give His life as a ransom for many [paying the price to set them free from the penalty of sin].*

A ransom was the price paid to release a slave from bondage. Jesus often told his disciples that He must die, but here He told them why—to redeem all people from the bondage of sin and death. The disciples thought that if Jesus was alive, He could save them. But Jesus revealed only His death would save them and the world.

Isaiah 61:1 says, *¹The Spirit of the Lord God is upon me, Because the Lord has anointed and commissioned me to bring Good News to the humble and afflicted; He has sent me to bind up [the wounds of] the brokenhearted, to proclaim release [from confinement and condemnation] to the [physical and spiritual] captives and freedom to prisoners...*

I am sure that my life is not too different from yours. My life has been full of questions, especially during hard times. All of us tend to ask questions such as "What is my purpose? Why was I created? How do I fit into God's bigger picture? Why do I experience the things that I do? How do I overcome these things? Will I ever be free?" Now don't get too excited because I cannot answer any of these questions for you, but I can share how I arrived at an answer for myself, which I believe will be encouraging to you.

Evidence of God's pursuit of us can be found in Psalm 139. Psalm 139 is one of the most powerful psalms in the entire Bible. This psalm comes from Kind David, its theme speaks to how God is all-seeing, all-knowing, all-powerful, and present everywhere. In this psalm we see that God knew us, God is with us, His greatest gift is to allow us to know Him and before we ever began to pursue Him, He pursued us.

I want to take a moment to encourage you in a few things from things from Psalm 139:

1. God knows the real you.—God knows everything about you. He knows everything about you and still sees you with unlimited worth. The beginning of Psalm 139 makes it clear

that God knows us better than we know ourselves. In verses 1-4 it says, *¹O Lord, You have searched me [thoroughly] and have known me. ²You know when I sit down and when I rise [my entire life, everything I do]; You understand my thoughts from afar. ³You scrutinize my path and my lying down, And You are intimately acquainted with all my ways. ⁴Even before there is a word on my tongue [still unspoken], Behold, O Lord, You know it all.*

Theologians talk about the fact that God is omniscient. This means that God knows everything, including the past, present, and future. Certainly, Psalm 139 affirms God's omniscience, but it seems like something deeper than omniscience is presented in this passage. God truly understands you. He knows your thoughts, history, fears, joys, and sorrows and amazingly, He still pursues you and you are still valuable to Him. God loves you fully, completely, and unconditionally!

Sometimes we don't let people get to know us completely because we are afraid, they will discover something about us that they won't like. But God already knows everything about us, even the number of hairs on our heads and still He accepts and loves us.

Matthew 10:29-31 says, *²⁹Are not two little sparrows sold for a copper coin? And yet not one of them falls to the ground apart from your Father's will. ³⁰But even the very hairs of your head are all numbered [for the Father is sovereign and has complete knowledge]. ³¹So do not fear; you are more valuable than many sparrows.*

Jesus said that God is aware of everything that happens even to sparrows, and you are far more valuable to Him than they are. You are so valuable to God that God sent His only Son to die for you. Because God places such value on you, you need never fear personal threats or difficult trials. These can't shake God's love or dislodge His Spirit from within you. But this doesn't mean that God will take away all your trouble. The real test of value is how well something holds up under the wear, tear, and abuse of everyday life. Those who stand up for Christ despite their troubles truly have lasting value and will receive great rewards. God is with us through every situation, in every trial—protecting, loving, guiding. He knows and loves us completely.

2. God is closer to you than you realize—Psalm 139 also shows us that wherever we are, God is there. In verses 7-8 it says, *⁷Where can I go from Your Spirit? Or where can I flee from Your presence? ⁸If I ascend to Heaven, You are there; If I make my bed in Sheol (the nether world, the place of the dead), behold, You are there.*

God is omnipresent—He is everywhere. Because this is so, you can never be lost to His Spirit. This is good news to those who know and love God, because no matter what we do or where we go, we can never be far from God's comforting presence. No matter where we are, in life or death, God is there. The psalmist says that we could travel to the other side of the earth, to the farthest oceans, but God would still be present.

Yet, as with omniscience, something more than a theological doctrine is discussed in these verses. It can be frightening to realize that we can't ever get away from God. Our sin tempts us to try and run away from God, but this is futile; because God is always near us and always wants to help us overcome and live in the freedom that Christ brought for us with His life.

3. God has always been at work in your life—If you just started to pursue God, it might feel like God is a new part of your life. However, the Bible makes it clear that God has been at work in your life since before you were born. In verses 13-16, it says, *¹³For You formed my innermost parts; You knit me [together] in my mother's womb. ¹⁴I will give thanks and praise to You, for I am fearfully and wonderfully made; Wonderful are Your works, and my soul knows it very well. ¹⁵My frame was not hidden from You, When I was being formed in secret, and intricately and skillfully formed [as if embroidered with many colors] in the depths of the earth. ¹⁶Your eyes have seen my*

unformed substance; And in Your book were all written the days that were appointed for me, when as yet there was not one of them [even taking shape].

God's character goes into the creation of every person. When you feel worthless or even begin to hate yourself, remember that God's Spirit is ready and willing to work within you. We should have as much respect for ourselves as our Maker has for us.

From conception to death, God has a plan for your life. God has put you on this earth to know Him, to honor Him, and to help others. And God has been pursuing you for your entire life. The clearest evidence is that He sent His son Jesus Christ to die for your sins on the cross. He did this, so you would truly know Him.

In this book, I want to share how, through hardships, I have come to know this wonderful God, and experience more of His presence in my life daily. As I stated before, the purpose of this book is to show you what freedom looks like and how to maintain it on the other side of overcoming. One thing God has placed a burden in my heart for is *aftercare*.

Cambridge Dictionary defines *aftercare* as the care of people after they have left a hospital or prison. *The church is not a harbor for saints; it is a hospital for sinners.* I read this phrase on social media. When we are sick and require hospitalization, all our needs are supplied until we are well enough to go home. But even once we get home, we must follow the doctors' orders until we are 100% healed. Even after we are 100% healed, there are things we need to do to maintain that healing. This is the picture of aftercare that many books, churches, ministries, and organizations are missing. It's great that 100 people gave their life to Christ during your program or after service, but these same people require aftercare. They need applicable *doctors'* orders to follow to continue their healing and after healing, deliverance, freedom and/or overcoming has taken place, there will always be things they need to do to maintain that.

So, in this book, you will read stories of things I have overcome as an encouragement for you to overcome, but more importantly, you will find prayers to initiate your freedom and applicable steps to maintain your freedom on the other side of overcoming.

****

In 2013, I turned 30 years old, and it had become a tradition among my family and friends that, on our birthday we share what we have learned over the past year and how God has blessed us. During my 30th birthday dinner, I decided to share my testimony with a few friends and family who were present.

This was the first time that I had shared my full testimony with any of them, including my mother. As I was sharing my testimony, God revealed something very powerful to me: *Everything I have experienced in life was so that I could bring glory, honor, and fame to His Name.*

Exodus 9:16 says, *But indeed for this very reason I have allowed you to live, in order to show you My power and in order that My name may be proclaimed throughout all the earth.* I have been in situations where I could have been killed, incarcerated or insane, BUT GOD spared me because HE had a purpose for my life. He had a purpose for my story, a story He knew would bring Him glory.

Proverbs 16:4 says, *The Lord has made everything for its own purpose, Even the wicked [according to their role] for the day of evil.* This verse doesn't mean that God created some people to be wicked, but rather God uses even the activities of the wicked people to fulfill His good purpose. God is infinite (limitless or endless), and we are finite (having limits or bounds). No matter how great our intellects are, we will never be able to understand Him completely. But we can accept by faith that He is all-powerful, all-loving and perfectly good. We can believe that He is not the cause of evil, and we can trust that there are no loose ends in His system of judgment. Evil is a temporary condition in this world. We often connect evil with our tests and trials, but one day God will destroy evil.

In the meantime, He uses the evil intentions of people for His good purpose.

That is so powerful. Knowing that God has a purpose for you even when life is hard, even when you feel like God has forgotten about you, when you are experiencing the worst pain or heartache that you think you could endure, God has not forsaken you. According to Merriam-Webster, the word *forsake* means to *renounce or turn away from entirely*. God will not renounce or turn away from you entirely. Deuteronomy 31:8 (NIV) says, *⁸The Lord Himself goes before you and will be with you; He will never leave you nor forsake you. Do not be afraid; do not be discouraged.*

God created you with a purpose and a plan to overcome, to help others overcome and lead others into the knowledge of Him. Romans 8:28-30 says, *²⁸And we know [with great confidence] that God [who is deeply concerned about us] causes all things to work together [as a plan] for good for those who love God, to those who are called according to His plan and purpose. ²⁹For those whom He foreknew [and loved and chose beforehand], He also predestined to be conformed to the image of His Son [and ultimately share in His complete sanctification], so that He would be the firstborn [the most beloved and honored] among many believers. ³⁰And those whom He predestined, He also called; and those whom He called, He also justified [declared free of the guilt of sin]; and those whom He justified, He also glorified [raising them to a Heavenly dignity].*

This verse embodies what God revealed to me on my 30th Birthday. Everything was predestined, because I am called, justified, and glorified in Christ. It is clear that God's purpose for us was not an afterthought; it was settled before the foundation of the world. Despite our circumstances, we are to serve and honor God. If you believe in Christ, you can rejoice in the fact that God has always known you. God's love is eternal. His wisdom and power are supreme. He will guide and protect you until you stand in His presence. That is how valuable you are to Him.

God works all things—not just isolated incidents—together for our good. This does not mean that all that happens to us *is* good. Evil is prevalent in our fallen world, but God can turn every circumstance around for our long-range good. God is not working to make us happy, but to fulfill His purpose. This promise is not for everybody. It can be claimed only by those who love God and are called according to His purpose. Those who are called are those the Holy Spirit convinces and enables to receive Christ. Such people have a new perspective, a new mindset on life. They trust in God, not life's treasures, they look for their security in Heaven, not on earth; they learn to accept not resent pain and persecution because God is with them.

No matter what happens to me God can use it. I am called according to God's purpose, but you may be thinking, *If God has a purpose for me, why do I have to suffer? Why does my life seem so hard?* I have asked myself those very same questions on numerous occasions. The answers can be found in verse 29 of Romans 8:28-30 (NLT) where it says, *For God knew His people in advance and He chose them to become like His Son...."*

God's goal for us is to make us like Christ. As we become more and more like Him, we discover our true selves, the men, and women of God we were created to be. How can we be conformed to Christ's likeness? By reading and heeding the Word, by studying His life on earth through the Gospels, by being filled with His Spirit, and by doing His work on the earth. The good news is, although Jesus suffered much; Jesus also overcame much so just as God chose you to be like His Son, God chose you to be an overcomer and live freely.

First John 3:2-3 says, *²Beloved, we are [even here and] now children of God, and it is not yet made clear what we will be [after His coming]. We know that when He comes and is revealed, we will [as His children] be like Him, because we will see Him just as He is [in all His glory]. ³And everyone who has this hope [confidently placed] in Him purifies himself, just as He is pure (holy, undefiled, guiltless).* This life is a process of becoming more and more like Christ. This process will not be complete until we see Christ face-to-face but knowing that it is our ultimate destiny should motivate us to purify ourselves. To purify means to keep morally straight, free from the corruption of sin. God also purifies us, but there is action we must take to remain morally fit.

That is encouraging. I must admit, I have not always believed the above statement, and that's what this book is about. This book is about the promise that God placed on my life before I was even born, before the foundation of the earth. Ephesians 1:3-6 paints a beautiful picture for us:

Ephesians 1:3 says, *Blessed and worthy of praise be the God and Father of our Lord Jesus Christ, who has blessed us with every spiritual blessing in the Heavenly realms in Christ, ...*

Who has blessed us with every spiritual blessing in the Heavenly realms means that in Christ we have all the benefits of knowing God—being chosen for salvation, being adopted as His children, forgiveness, insight, the gifts of the Spirit, power to do God's will, and the hope of living forever with Christ. Because we have an intimate relationship with Christ, we can enjoy these blessings now. The *Heavenly realms* means that these blessings are eternal, not temporal. These blessings come from Christ's spiritual realm, not the earthly realm.

Ephesians 1:4 says, *...just as [in His love] He chose us in Christ [actually selected us for Himself as His own] before the foundation of the world, so that we would be holy [that is, consecrated, set apart for Him, purpose-driven] and blameless in His sight.*

The Apostle Paul says that God *chose us in Him* to emphasize that salvation depends totally on God. We are not saved because we deserve it, but because God is gracious and freely gives salvation. We did not influence God's decision to save us; He saved us according to His plan. Thus, there is no way to take credit for our salvation or to allow room for pride. The mystery of salvation originated in the timeless mind of God long before we existed. It is hard to understand how God can accept us. But because of Christ, we are holy and blameless in His sight. God chose us, and when we belong to Him through Jesus Christ, God looks at us as if we never sinned. All we can do is express our thanks for His wonderful love.

Ephesians 1:5 says, *He predestined and lovingly planned for us to be adopted to Himself as [His own] children through Jesus Christ, in accordance with the kind intention and good pleasure of His will—...* Ephesians 1:11-12 declares, *¹¹In Him also we have [a]received an inheritance [a destiny—we were claimed by God as His own], having been predestined (chosen, appointed beforehand) according to the purpose of Him who works everything in agreement with the counsel and design of His will,*

¹²so that we who were the first to hope in Christ [who first put our confidence in Him as our Lord and Savior] would exist to the praise of His glory.

The words translated *predestined* in the Scriptures referenced above are from the Greek word *proorizo*, which carries the meaning of *determining beforehand, ordaining,* or *deciding ahead of time.* So, predestination is God determining certain things to occur ahead of time. What did God decide ahead of time? God predetermined that certain individuals would be conformed to the likeness of His Son, be called, justified, and glorified. Numerous Scriptures refer to believers in Christ being chosen, such as Matthew 24:22, 31; Mark 13:20, 27; Romans 8:33, 9:11, 11:5-7, 28; Ephesians 1:11; Colossians 3:12; 1 Thessalonians 1:4; 1 Timothy 5:21; 2 Timothy 2:10; Titus 1:1; 1 Peter 1:1-2, 2:9; and 2 Peter 1:10. Predestination is the biblical doctrine that God in His sovereignty chooses certain individuals to be saved. This is another way of saying that salvation is God's work and not our own doing. Many people have a strong hostility to the doctrine of predestination. However, predestination is a Biblical doctrine. The key is understanding what predestination means, biblically.

In His infinite love, God has chosen and adopted us as His own children. Through Jesus' sacrifice, He has brought us into His family and made us heirs along with Jesus.

Romans 8:17 says, *And if [we are His] children, [then we are His] heirs also: heirs of God and fellow heirs with Christ [sharing His spiritual blessing and inheritance], if indeed we share in His suffering so that we may also share in His glory.*

In Roman law, adopted children had the same rights and privileges as biological children, even if they had been slaves. Paul uses this term to show how strong our relationship to God is.

Ephesians 1:6 says, *...to the praise of His glorious grace and favor, which He so freely bestowed on us in the Beloved [His Son, Jesus Christ]. Freely bestowed on us in the Beloved* means that God graciously accepts us (though we don't deserve it) now that we belong to His dearly loved Son.

We all were born with a promise, and that promise is proof from God that we are born to overcome. Before we see the promise come to fruition, we see the pain and the process of overcoming Satan's attacks first. The pain is what you must endure in life for God to develop, grow and transform you. This is the stage where we may or may not know God or have a close relationship with Him, so everything in life seems hard. We constantly ask, "Why me?" and feel sorry for ourselves, our situations, and our circumstances.

The process begins when we realize that everything in our lives that has occurred has happened for a reason. This is the time that we begin to look beyond our lives, beyond our little world and see God's bigger picture. Think of it this way, our lives are like 4x6 pictures, all we see in our own picture is ourselves, our problems, our worries, our family, our jobs, our friends and so on. God's picture is so big that I cannot put a number on it and our little 4x6 picture is just one very small part of His big picture! When you think in those terms, you begin to see that although our picture is small, we fit into God's picture, and we all have a place. When your perspective changes, you begin to walk in and fulfill the promise that God has placed on your life. We are purposed to live the life of freedom God promised to us through His Son Jesus. When sin entered the world, we forgot we were overcomers, so we must be reminded how to overcome, and we do that through Christ, by renewing our minds in God's Word and by applying God's Word to our lives.

In my 40 years of life, I have learned that life is all about perspective. It's not about what you see, but it's about how you perceive what you see. If you choose to see life and life's struggles through the lenses that you've been an overcomer since birth, what you go through will become so much easier to go through because your attitude will be one of faith in God and not one of woe is me. I promise! But I caution you, it is a process, and for me it did not happen overnight. As you read though this book, I pray you are challenged to discover the promises of God for you. I pray you begin overcoming the attacks of Satan daily. I pray your perspective will be forever changed, and at the end of this book you will believe you can live in freedom on the other side of *overcoming*.

My Prayer for You:

Father God, I pray for each person holding this book. I know You did not allow them to purchase or receive this book by coincidence because everything You allow, has a purpose! So, Father God, I lay them at Your Feet today. I pray that the eyes of the hearts of each reader may be enlightened, so they will know what the hope of Your calling is, what are the riches of the Glory of Your inheritance in the saints, and what is the surpassing greatness of Your power toward us who believe. I pray their spiritual ears will open to receive revelation as they read the words You have inspired in these pages. Father God, meet them where they are and bring them into a greater understanding of who You are and why You allow the things You do. In the matchless, strong name of my Lord and Savior Jesus Christ I pray, Amen.

Prologue

This will be a time and an opportunity for you to testify [about Me]. *Luke 21:13*

Psalm 22:22 says, *I will tell of Your name to my brethren; In the midst of the assembly, I will praise You.* David would praise God in the assembly because his private deliverance deserved a public testimony. God wonderfully delivers us from bondage in the quiet moments when we are hurting, and we must be prepared to offer public praise for His care. That's what God did for me, and I simply desire to honor the Lord by bearing witness to His work in my life.

The Lord commends sharing testimonies throughout His Word, particularly in the Psalms. We continually read of the Psalmist promising to tell of the greatness of the Lord *In the midst of the assembly*. Often, he asks the Lord to deliver him so that he can testify of God's salvation. The Bible is filled with the most powerful stories we will ever read or hear, but it isn't just a storybook! It is God's testimony to each of us. We are all part of God's story. As Christians we are to repeat the story of God's love to others who need to hear it. That includes the nations around the world, the neighbors across the street, and every person like you who will read this book.

In 1 John 1:1-4, it says, *¹[I am writing about] what existed from the beginning, what we have heard, what we have seen with our eyes, what we have looked at and touched with our hands, concerning the Word of Life [the One who existed even before the beginning of the world, Christ]— ²and the Life [an aspect of His being] was manifested, and we have seen [it as eyewitnesses] and testify and declare to you [the Life], the eternal Life who was [already existing] with the Father and was [actually] made visible to us [His followers]— ³what we have seen and heard we also proclaim to you, so that you too may have fellowship [as partners] with us. And indeed, our fellowship [which is a distinguishing mark of born-again believers] is with the Father, and with His Son Jesus Christ. ⁴We are writing these things to you so that our joy [in seeing you included] may be made complete [by having you share in the joy of salvation].*

Did you catch the word, "testify" in the Scripture from above? I grew up watching a lot of TV, especially crime dramas. I am a big fan of *whodunit...* movies and TV shows. With most there is always bound to be a courtroom scene where someone is being sworn in. If I've heard the swearing in of one witness, I've heard it 100 times. "Do you solemnly swear that the testimony that you are about to give is the truth, the whole truth and nothing but the truth, so help you God?" What does this tell us? That I watched too much TV? Yes, but it also tells us something about giving a testimony. We are to tell the truth!

In this passage we find that John, who walked with Jesus, was sharing that story with his readers. He was testifying, announcing the Good News of Jesus to those who would listen. As an eyewitness to Jesus' ministry, John was qualified to teach the truth about Him. The readers of this letter had not seen and heard Jesus themselves, but they could trust what John wrote was accurate. We are like those second- and third-generation Christians. Though we have not personally seen, heard, or touched Jesus, we have the New Testament record of His eyewitnesses, and we can trust they spoke the truth about Him (see John 20:29).

John also writes about having fellowship with other believers. There are three principles behind true Christian fellowship. First, our fellowship is grounded in the testimony of God's Word. Without this underlying strength, togetherness is impossible. Second, it is mutual, depending on the unity of believers. Third, it is renewed daily through the Holy Spirit. True fellowship combines social and spiritual interaction, and it is made possible through a living relationship with Christ.

There is something else we need to understand about testimony. It is about what we know to be the truth...not what we think or what we have heard. It is all about what we know! That's exactly what God expects from each of His followers— to simply share what we know—to testify to others of what

God has done in our lives; to what we have seen Him do in our lives. We don't have to have the Bible memorized or be able to answer every question that someone might have about God. We only have to be willing to share the story of what God did in our lives!

During His time on earth that's exactly what happened. Jesus would work in someone's life, and they would simply share that story with others. In the New Testament, the Gospels and the book of Acts provide us with many examples of men and women who testify about what Jesus has done for them. Here are three:

1. In John 9:24-25, when Jesus healed the blind man:
²⁴So a second time they called the man who had been [born] blind, and said to him, "Give God glory and praise [for your sight]! We know this Man [Jesus] is a sinner [separated from God]." ²⁵Then he answered, "I do not know whether He is a sinner [separated from God]; but one thing I do know, that though I was blind, now I see.

By now the man who was blind had heard the same questions over and over by the Pharisees. He did not know how or why he was healed, but he knew that his life had been miraculously changed, and he was not afraid to tell the truth. You don't need to know all the answers to share Christ with others. It is important to tell how He has changed your life.

Then trust that God will use your words to help others believe in Him too!

2. In John 4:29, when Jesus forgave the Samaritan woman: *"Come, see a man who told me all the things that I have done! Can this be the Christ (the Messiah, the Anointed)?"*

3. In John 4:42, when many Samaritans believe in Jesus ...*and they told the woman, "We no longer believe just because of what you said; for [now] we have heard Him for ourselves and know [with confident assurance] that this One is truly the Savior of [all] the world."*

The disciples were simply ordinary men who told people the extraordinary story of Jesus working in their lives. That was what Jesus wanted them to do, it's what He wants us to do and it's what I've done in this book.

²⁷But you will testify also and be My witnesses because you have been with Me from the beginning.
John 15:27

Remember, the saints in Revelation 12:11 are said to have overcome Satan *by the blood of the Lamb and by the word of their testimony*. Whatever the exact nature of this testimony, we know they were publicly identifying with Jesus Christ despite the opposition of Satan.

A principle emerges across the pages of Scripture: one of God's design in saving us is that we will, in turn, honor Him by sharing our testimony with others.

The world needs Christians who will not be afraid to live their faith and share their testimony. Mark 16:15 says, *And He said to them, "Go into all the world and preach the gospel to all creation.* We will not be able to do that unless we realize the power and importance of our testimony.

Come and hear, all who fear God [and worship Him with awe-inspired reverence and obedience], And I will tell what He has done for me. Psalm 66:16

Chapter One

Overcoming Negative Thinking: Breaking Free from the Bad Habit

For as he thinks in his heart, so is he [in behavior—one who manipulates].
Proverbs 23:7a

According to Merriam-Webster, a habit is defined as an acquired mode of behavior that has become nearly or completely involuntary. Negative thinking is a bad habit that has been developed over time that needs to be broken for us to live as free, victorious overcomers.

According to Dr. Rita Schulte, author of *Think This, Not That*, the most common types of negative thoughts include the following:

1. Should, must, ought to be, and must be statements: These inflexible beliefs are based on misperceptions and can lead to anxiety, depression, self-pity, anger, and guilt.

2. Jumping to conclusions, mind reading, and fortune telling (thinking we know what will happen): These patterns interpret situations and outcomes based on distortions, fears, and beliefs.

3. Overgeneralization: This cognitive distortion happens when we assume that because something happened one way it will always happen that way. We can recognize this thinking pattern by words like never, always, and everyone.

4. Personalization: When we see things as our fault without recognizing other contributing factors, we are personalizing. People who personalize see the issue as something wrong with themselves, a character flaw or deficit. It often cycles into personal name calling (*I'm an idiot, I'm a loser, I'm unlovable*) and self-condemnation.

5. Disqualifying the positive: Schulte explains this pattern, *Disqualifying the positive is a way we overestimate a negative outcome and minimize our ability to cope with difficult situations. We reject our positive experiences, or our strengths, and we focus instead on the negative aspects of our situation or our character.*

6. Catastrophizing: Imagining the worst and blowing things out of proportion are typical of catastrophizing thoughts. This kind of thinking provokes anxiety, focusing on what ifs and fears.

7. Emotional reasoning: Interpreting negative feelings as truth is a destructive pattern of unhealthy thinking. I feel unworthy becomes a belief that I am unworthy.

8. All or nothing thinking. This pattern moves from one extreme to another, not recognizing the middle ground between. For example, feeling inadequate may lead to the belief I must be perfect or I'm a total failure.

9. Externalizing: The opposite of personalizing, externalizing blames others or situations without acknowledging any role or responsibility in the issue. We find a biblical example of externalizing in Matthew 7:3, when Jesus asks, *³Why do you look at the [insignificant] speck that is in your brother's eye, but do not notice and acknowledge the [egregious] log that is in your own eye?*

10. Magnifying/minimizing: Making a mountain out of a molehill is a type of magnifying thoughts. On the opposite extreme is minimizing situations, feelings, pain, problems, offenses. Again, Dr. Schulte helpfully explains the problem with minimizing: *Here you shrink the importance of things, such as your feelings when you're hurt, saying they don't really matter, for one reason or the other. This is often known as the martyr complex. Comparing yourself or what you're going through with what someone else is feeling is another way to open the door for minimizing. It's healthy to feel your feelings when you have them. Minimizing does your pain a disservice.*

Learning to identify negative thinking is the first step to overcoming this mental trap. Pay attention to your thoughts, and don't give negative thoughts free reign. Well, try not to because it's a challenge, for sure.

For close to 30 years negative thoughts consumed me in every way and often led to sins that I may not have committed if I would've captured the thoughts and brought them into the obedience of Christ immediately. To overcome negative thinking, you must learn how to quickly put the thought beside the Word of God to see if it matches. If it doesn't match you have to cast it down right away! I found many of my thoughts were driven by the world and not the Word of God, which was a bad habit that kept me from living my full potential for Christ.

Evangelist, Joyce Meyer, referred to the mind as a battlefield and that is 100% true! The way we think shapes what we believe and vice versa. Satan often has a field day in the minds and hearts of believers. I was one of those believers that he had a grand ole time with.

I decided to start with negative thinking because sin starts with a thought that is not captured. I believe that we are often defeated and never even try to overcome because we believe the first thought that enters our mind about our situations. We all know the quote, *"Watch your thoughts; they become words. Watch your words; they become actions. Watch your* actions; they become habit. Watch your habits; they become character. Watch your character; it becomes your destiny."

Almost every struggle I talk about in this book started with a thought. Thoughts are like bubbles, when you first blow a bubble, you're able to capture it quickly but if you don't it will become out of reach. This is how negative thoughts should be handled, as soon as you think it, capture it. That is what we are being instructed to do in 2 Corinthians 10:3-6 where it says, *³For though we walk in the flesh [as mortal men], we are not carrying on our [spiritual] warfare according to the flesh and using the weapons of man. ⁴The weapons of our warfare are not physical [weapons of flesh and blood]. Our weapons are divinely powerful for the destruction of fortresses. ⁵We are destroying sophisticated arguments and every exalted and proud thing that sets itself up against the [true] knowledge of God, and we are taking every thought and purpose captive to the obedience of Christ, ⁶being ready to punish every act of disobedience, when your own obedience [as a church] is complete.*

We are merely weak humans like Paul, but we don't need to use human plans and methods to win our battles. God's' mighty weapons are available to us as we fight against Satan on the battlefield of our minds. Christians must choose whose methods to use, God's or the world's. Paul assures us that God's mighty weapons—prayer, faith, hope love, God's Word, the Holy Spirit—are powerful and effective!

Ephesians 6:13-18 says, *¹³Therefore, put on the complete armor of God, so that you will be able to [successfully] resist and stand your ground in the evil day [of danger], and having done everything [that the crisis demands], to stand firm [in your place, fully prepared, immovable, victorious]. ¹⁴So stand firm and hold your ground, having tightened the wide band of truth (personal integrity, moral courage) around your waist and having put on the breastplate of righteousness (an upright heart), ¹⁵and having strapped on your feet the gospel of peace in preparation [to face the enemy with firm-footed stability and the readiness produced by the Good News]. ¹⁶Above all, lift up the [protective] shield of faith with which you can extinguish all the flaming arrows of the evil one. ¹⁷And take the helmet of salvation, and the sword of the Spirit, which is the Word of God. ¹⁸With all prayer and petition pray [with specific requests] at all times [on every occasion and in every season] in the Spirit, and with this in view, stay alert with all perseverance and petition [interceding in prayer] for all God's people.*

Using the Armor of God is how we fight the battle in our minds. In the Christian life, we battle against rulers and spiritual forces (the powerful evil forces of fallen angels headed by Satan, who is a vicious fighter.) To withstand their attacks, we must depend on God's' strength and use every piece of His armor. Those who are not *flesh and blood* are demons, over whom Satan has control. They are not mere fantasies—they are very real and wage war against us in our thoughts. We face a powerful army whose goal is to defeat Christ's' chosen. When we believe in Christ, these beings become our enemies, and they try every device to turn us away from Him and back to sin. One of these devices is whispering lies to us. Although we are assured of victory, we must engage in the struggle until Christ returns. We need supernatural power to defeat Satan, and God has provided this by giving us His Holy Spirit within us and His armor surrounding us. God has equipped you with everything you need to break the habit of negative thinking.

The weapons mentioned in 2 Corinthians 10:3-6, can break down the proud human arguments against God and the walls that Satan builds to keep people from finding God, often planted as thoughts. When dealing with the pride that keeps people from a relationship with Christ, we may be tempted to use our own methods. But nothing can break down these barriers in our thoughts like God's weapons.

Now let's pay attention to verse 5 where it says *we are taking every thought and purpose captive to the obedience of Christ.* Our thoughts should obey Christ! Paul uses military terminology to describe this warfare against sin and Satan. God must be the Commander-in-Chief, even our thoughts must be submitted to His control as we live for Him. Spirit-empowered believers must capture every thought and yield it to Christ. When exposed to ideas or opportunities that might lead to wrong desires, you have a choice. You can recognize the danger and turn away, or you can allow unhealthy thoughts to take you captive. You capture your fantasies and desires when you honestly admit them to the Lord and ask Him to redirect your thinking. Ask God to give you the spirit of discernment to keep your thoughts focused on His truth.

To capture our thoughts is to recognize and notice them, and it is also refusing to let negative thoughts run wild, build walls, define identities, or drive decisions. Capturing is surrendering thoughts to Christ rather than letting them fester, entrench or ingrain themselves in our mind.

We bring Christ into the negative when we entrust our thoughts to Him. In *Switch on Your Brain: The Key to Peak Happiness, Thinking, and Health*, Dr. Caroline Leaf explains that when we do this, something amazing happens both spiritually and physically. Harnessing negative thought, changing it through awareness, repentance, and forgiveness, and replacing it with truth helps rewire healthy new circuits in our brains, part of God's transforming work in our minds.

I believe a thought it is how Eve fell in the Garden; the serpent deposited seeds of lies to change her thinking. Let's read Genesis 3:1-6:

¹Now the serpent was more crafty (subtle, skilled in deceit) than any living creature of the field which the Lord God had made. And the serpent (Satan) said to the woman, "Can it really be that God has said, 'You shall not eat from any tree of the garden'?" ²And the woman said to the serpent, "We may eat fruit from the trees of the garden, ³except the fruit from the tree which is in the middle of the garden. God said, 'You shall not eat from it nor touch it, otherwise you will die.'" ⁴But the serpent said to the woman, "You certainly will not die! ⁵For God knows that on the day you eat from it your eyes will be opened [that is, you will have greater awareness], and you will be like God, knowing [the difference between] good and evil." ⁶And when the woman saw that the tree was good for food, and that it was delightful to look at, and a tree to be desired in order to make one wise and insightful, she took some of its fruit and ate it; and she also gave some to her husband with her, and he ate.

Do you see what happened here? We all know what God said about The Tree of the Knowledge of Good and Evil in Genesis 2:16-17, *¹⁶And the Lord God commanded the man, saying, "You may freely (unconditionally) eat [the fruit] from every tree of the garden; ¹⁷but [only] from the tree of the knowledge (recognition) of good and evil you shall not eat, otherwise on the day that you eat from it, you shall most certainly die [because of your disobedience]."* God said don't eat it, but the serpent convinced her that it was okay. The word convinced means to be completely certain about something or firm in one's belief. Satan planted a seed in her mind that made her rethink what

God had commanded. If she would have only remembered God's Words and cast down the thought immediately when it was introduced, then maybe sin would not have entered the world.

As a side note, why would God place a tree in the garden and then forbid Adam to eat from it? God wanted Adam to obey, but God gave Adam the freedom to choose. Without choice, Adam would have been like a prisoner, and his obedience would've been hollow. The two trees provided an exercise in choice, with rewards for choosing to obey and sad consequences for choosing to disobey. When you're faced with a choice in your thoughts, choose to obey God every single time.

God hasn't changed and neither has the enemy. Satan is the same and still up to his old tricks, which is why 2 Corinthians 2:11 tells us *to keep Satan from taking advantage of us; for we are not ignorant of his schemes.* All the different stories told in this book are directly related to how I used to think.

Romans 12:1-2 (NASB) says, *¹Therefore I urge you, brothers, and sisters, by the mercies of God, to present your bodies [dedicating all of yourselves, set apart] as a living sacrifice, holy and well-pleasing to God, which is your rational (logical, intelligent) act of worship. ²And do not be conformed to this world [any longer with its superficial values and customs] but be transformed and progressively changed [as you mature spiritually] by the renewing of your mind [focusing on godly values and ethical attitudes], so that you may prove [for yourselves] what the will of God is, that which is good and acceptable and perfect [in His plan and purpose for you].*

When sacrificing an animal according to God's law, a priest would kill the animal, cut it in pieces, and place it on the alter. Sacrifice was important, but even the Old Testament God made it clear that obedience from the heart was much more important (see 1 Samuel 15:22; Psalm 40:6; and Amos 5:21-24). God wants us to offer ourselves, not animals, as living sacrifices—daily laying aside our own desires to follow Him, putting all our energy and resources at His disposal and trusting Him to guide us. We do this out of gratitude that our sins have been forgiven.

God has good, acceptable, and perfect plans for His children. He wants us to be transformed people with renewed minds, living to honor and obey Him. He wants only what is best for us and He gave His Son to make our new lives possible, so we should joyfully give ourselves as living sacrifices for His service. Christians are called to *not be conformed to this world*, with its behavior and customs that are usually selfish and often corrupt. Many Christians wisely decide that much worldly behavior is off limits for them. Our refusal to conform to this world's values, however, must go even deeper than the level of behavior and customs—it must be firmly planted in our minds—*be transformed by the renewing of your mind*. It is possible to avoid most worldly customs and still be proud, covetous, selfish, stubborn, and arrogant. Only when the Holy Spirit renews, re-educates, and redirects our minds are we truly transformed.

Romans 8:5-8 says, *⁵For those who are living according to the flesh set their minds on the things of the flesh [which gratify the body], but those who are living according to the Spirit, [set their minds on] the things of the Spirit [His will and purpose]. ⁶Now the mind of the flesh is death [both now and forever—because it pursues sin]; but the mind of the Spirit is life and peace [the spiritual well-being that comes from walking with God—both now and forever]; ⁷the mind of the flesh [with its sinful pursuits] is actively hostile to God. It does not submit itself to God's law, since it cannot, ⁸and those who are in the flesh [living a life that caters to sinful appetites and impulses] cannot please God.*

In this passage of Scripture, Paul divides people into two categories—those who let themselves be controlled by their sinful natures, and those who follow the Holy Spirit. All of us would be in the first category if Jesus hadn't offered us a way out. Once we have said yes to Jesus, we will want to continue following Him, because His way brings life and peace. Daily we must consciously choose to center our lives and thoughts on God. We must use the Bible to discover God's guidelines for our thoughts and then follow them. In every perplexing situation ask yourself, "What would Jesus want me to do?" When the Holy Spirit points out what is right, do it eagerly.

I've overcome rape, lust, sickness, health challenges, bullying, low self-esteem, depression, self-pity, poor body image, jealousy, envy, ungratefulness, low self-confidence, and unforgiveness just to name a few. Most of which began in my thoughts. So, how did I overcome these things and break the bad habit of negative thinking? First, I recognized what I was thinking was not right and, quite often, not godly. Secondly, I began to read God's Word to see what the truth was and lastly, I began to meditate on and apply these Biblical truths in my life until I believed them.

To overcome negative thinking, you must KNOW 2 Corinthians 10:4-6, and you must DO Ephesians 6:10-17. I want to pay attention to one specific piece of armor mentioned in Ephesians, The Helmet of Salvation. In a battle, soldiers usually get injured and many times, the injuries are life-threatening. A soldier might survive a broken arm, but an injury to the head can be fatal! See where I am going here? See the importance of protecting and guarding your head? The head covers our minds, and our minds are the battlefield where spiritual warfare is waged. Our minds and thoughts are the top priority point of attack for the enemy. Therefore, it becomes imperative that we wear protective headgear to safeguard our minds. As you can see in Ephesians 6, God provided us with The Helmet of Salvation as protection for our minds. But wait, what exactly is The Helmet of Salvation? The Helmet of Salvation is the hope of salvation, the hope of salvation from Hell and salvation from sin.

The importance of hope can be seen in our everyday lives. Workers will put all their energy into their jobs in the hope that their efforts will be noticed and result in material rewards. Should they lose their job, it is the hope that they will get a better one. Take away the hope of gaining profitable employment and you would have effectively incapacitated them. They will find themselves sitting at home in despair. Take away their hope in life itself, and you would have destroyed that worker completely. Do you see the connection between hope and our thoughts? Let me give you an example:

March 16, 2012, I started a course to help me prepare to take an examination to earn my A+ Certification (Computer Technician Certification). I'd always been good with computers and repairing them but never had formal training before. I worked my way through the course and finished in August of 2012. I graduated at the top of my class, but the real test was coming when I would sit for the examination, and I was nervous.

The CompTIA A+ examination was two parts, both having more than 50 questions each. It was recommended that you take part one, then come back and take part two, but me being the optimistic person I am, I decided to take both parts back-to-back on August 18, 2012. I can still remember how anxious I was, but I kept telling myself, I had to pass because I was not about to let $358.00 go to waste. I took part one and passed, then had a quick break before taking part two, which was more intensive. I used the break time to study. I went back in and took part two and passed as well. August 18, 2012, was a good day! I remember crying in the car, I also remember I called a friend on the way home to tell her the good news, and she cried as well. Passing these tests and receiving my A+ Certification meant that I could start applying for entry-level jobs in the IT field which was much more lucrative than the mental health field, where I was currently working. I was super excited!

I began to apply at different places, but none of my experience was professional. One day in early March of 2013 I received a call from an old friend who had just been hired on a federal government contract. He had been hired as the Service Desk Manager and was given the freedom to build his own team. He instructed me to go to the website and apply for the job. I was called in for an interview the next week. The week after, I received an offer letter. Two weeks after I signed my offer letter, I started working on the Service Desk, which was April 1, 2013.

In my mind, I had arrived. I was earning double what I made at my previous job, and I was loving my work. I got to learn so many new things and use the previous experience I'd gained over the years just by tinkering with things and fixing the computers of my friends and family. I was a hard worker, and I expected my hard work to pay off. Everything was going smoothly until I found out that the contract I'd been hired on was up for a rebid. For those who don't know, a rebid occurs when the current contract is nearing its end and the client opens the contract to other companies.

I was upset to find this out, but I was confident that if the company I currently worked for lost the contract, I would be picked up by the new company because I was a hard worker. I had hope. I continued working hard, working overtime, and going above and beyond my duties and eventually, my hard work did pay off.

In September of 2013 my Team Lead was offered a job at another company, so that meant her position was about to be available. She told me she was going to recommend me for the Team Lead position, but before she could even recommend me, the Service Desk manager offered me the position. I accepted. I received an $11,000.00 raise, and I was elated. I was now making more money than I had ever made in my entire life! Unfortunately, the company I worked for lost the bid, but during the transition process, I continued to work hard in the hopes that the new company who won the bid would recognize that I was an asset and hire me on the new contract.

Like all jobs, we had to go through an interview process for the new company. In the interview, I was pretty much told I was going to be brought onto the new contract because they felt I had the experience and knowledge needed to advance the contract. As a result, I never looked for another job. Unfortunately, I made the mistake of putting my trust in man.

Psalm 118:8 says, *It is better to take refuge in the Lord than to trust in man.* Pilots put confidence in their planes. Commuters place confidence in trains, cars, or buses. Each day we must put our confidence in something or someone. If you are willing to trust a plane or car to get you to your destination, are you willing to trust God to guide you here on earth? Do you trust Him more than any human being? These are all questions I had to ask myself. How futile (useless, vain, worthless) is it to trust anything or anyone more than God.

A couple weeks later I found out that the new contract for the Service Desk department was going to be in Knoxville, Tennessee. I was working in Fairfax, Virginia at the time and

Tennessee was far away, but I remained hopeful that there would be remote jobs available. Two days after finding out the contract was moving to Tennessee, the new Service Desk Manager called me and offered me a job as a Service Desk Team Lead on the new team. I was so excited but accepting this job would mean moving to Tennessee and taking a $15,000.00 pay cut.

I was devastated. I did consider moving, but the move would not have been beneficial to me in any way, and the company gave me no reason to move, other than the fact that I would have a job and there was no state income tax in Tennessee. The Service Desk Manager really tried to persuade me, but I would've had more duties than I currently had with less pay. I was so upset with God! Why would You allow me to get this job, be promoted and make all this money, only to take it away after a few short months. I was planning to have a townhouse built, but in an instant, my plans changed because I was unsure of my financial future or if I'd be able to afford the house. Thank God, I had not signed any contracts yet.

Despite being upset and turning down the offer to move to Tennessee I was confident I was still a good employee, and I was determined the new company was going to see that and pick me up to work remotely from the DC area. I composed a proposal, detailing how much of an asset I was and how having remote workers was a benefit to a company. To this day, I have never received a response to my proposal, even after training all the Tennessee employees that were flown in. The end of the contract came and as of January 31, 2014, I became unemployed. Again, I was devastated. How could they do me like that?

I didn't know what to do. I had to pray and seek God, even though I felt like I had been slighted by Him. I still chose to seek Him. That first week in February God placed it in my heart to start my own IT business and on February 14, 2014, I filed the LLC. When the paperwork came back saying I was official, I cried. I cried because it was a victory after what I perceived as a defeat. I cried because the approval was a second chance for me. I cried because I no longer felt like a failure. I cried because I had hope again.

I dedicated that business to God and since then He has provided all my needs. I have told you all this to show that hope and our thoughts are connected. Hope combined with our thoughts can change our perspective. Therefore, the Helmet of Salvation is so important and a vital piece of armor.

The word for hope in the Greek is Elpis, (el-peace) and the translation literally means confident expectation. The confident expectation we must have of the day when Jesus Christ will return, therefore fulfilling all the promises made in The Word of God. On that day the work that He began in us when we were born again will be completed and we will secure eternal life. Which is why we must be careful where we place our hope. In my story, I placed all my hope in myself, my work ethic, and in the leaders at this new company, thinking they would see how hard of a worker I was and bring me onto the new contract when really my hope should've been in the Lord from the very beginning.

Isaiah 40:31 says, *But those who wait for the Lord [who expect, look for, and hope in Him] Will gain new strength and renew their power; They will lift up their wings [and rise up close to God] like eagles [rising toward the sun]; They will run and not become weary, they will walk and not grow tired.*

Hoping in the Lord is expecting that His promise of strength will help us to rise above life's distractions and difficulties. It also means trusting in God. Trusting helps us to be prepared when He speaks to us. Then we will be patient when He asks us to wait and expect Him to fulfill the promises found in His Word.

It is the hope of eternal life that can protect our mind from the relentless attacks of the enemy. A Christian who has this hope will not get confused with the pleasures of sin; they won't trade their salvation for the temporary lusts of the world; they won't worry or be anxious about life's tests and trials, either. When the enemy shoots his arrows, they will not succumb, because their defenses will be secure in our Lord and Savior Jesus Christ, who has equipped us with the weapons of our warfare.

The enemy is constantly whispering in the ears of believers asking why we are choosing to sacrifice the pleasures of life that are so freely and readily available to us. The enemy's beckoning is always played to the accompanying tune of little white lies or half-truths. Admittedly at times, (particularly when I am weak,) the temptation to buy into the enemies lies seem impossible to resist. What stops me from giving in is knowing that what he offers is temporary, while what God promises is forever, and my hope is that if I cling to His promise, I will attain it.

Let's revisit Eve in the Garden again for a moment. Notice two things I just said above: "The enemies beckoning is always played to the accompanying tune of little white lies or half-truths" and "What stops me from giving in is knowing that what he offers is temporary..." Satan tries to lead us into sin by attacking our thoughts through little white lies, half-truths, and temporal things. Satan knows the Word of God just as we do, and he used it in a twisted way to distort what God told Eve as we saw in Genesis 3:1. You can see where he twisted God's words and made Eve second guess what God said; at that very moment is when 2 Corinthians 10:5 should've been activated.

When the enemy whispers something in your ear or tries to plant a negative thought, you must bring that thought into the obedience of Christ. That thought must be captured immediately and compared against (submitted to) the Word of God and if it doesn't line up, it must be cast down! Hope develops the same way faith develops, and like the Shield of Faith, the Helmet of Salvation grows stronger with use. According to Ginger Harrington, one strategy we should use to combat negative thinking is prayer. Pray for God's help for breaking ingrained thought patterns. Prayer is a powerful practice for overcoming our tendency to dwell on the negative. Many negative thought patterns run under the radar of our awareness and are often habitual patterns that can be hard to harness. God is the one who does the heavy lifting in transforming our thoughts. A simple strategy is to ask Christ to empower you to recognize negative thoughts and to make a better choice. In the moment, rely on Christ to help you to choose to break the cycle of negative thinking by remembering:

- To replace doubt with faith.
- To rely on the Spirit rather than default to old patterns of the flesh.
- To focus on good instead of evil.
- To focus on love rather than animosity.
- To focus on trust instead of anxiety.

- To focus on forgiveness rather than bitterness and resentment.
- To focus on right instead of wrong and
- Purity over immorality.

Ephesians 6:18 says, *With all prayer and petition pray [with specific requests] at all times [on every occasion and in every season] in the Spirit, and with this in view, stay alert with all perseverance and petition [interceding in prayer] for all God's people.* How can anyone always pray? One way is to make quick brief prayers your habitual response to every thought and situation you meet throughout the day. For example, each time a negative or impure thought comes to mind, turn it immediately to prayer:

Father God in Heaven, thank You that Your Holy Spirit lives in me. By His power, I have victory over this thought. Replace it now with the truth. In Jesus's name, Amen.

Then recite a Scripture or sing a song of praise to put your mind where it ought to be—focused on the Lord and things of God.

Remember Provers 23: 7a (NASB), *For as he thinks [reckons in his soul] within himself, so he is.*

Another way is to order your life around God's desires and teachings so that your very life becomes a prayer. You don't have to isolate yourself from other people and from daily work to pray constantly. You can make prayer your life and your life a prayer while living in a world that needs God's powerful influence. Praying "for all the saints" means praying for all believers in Christ; so, pray for the Christians you know and for the church around the world.

To overcome and break the bad habit of negative thinking the first step is to retrain your thinking and renew your thoughts through the Word of God and be prepared for attacks by wearing the Helmet of Salvation. Just as God has equipped us with armor for the battle, God also gave you everything that you need to overcome negative thoughts and break free from the bad habit.

Steps to Overcome Negative Thinking
1. Identify sources of negativity (see 1 John 2:15-16).
2. Take every thought captive (see 2 Corinthians 10:5).
3. Renew your mind (see Roman 12:2).
4. Cultivate thankfulness (see Philippians 4:6-7).
5. Worship (see Psalm 95:1-6).

Credit: https://rosilindjukic.com/5-biblical-steps-to-overcome-negative-thinking/

A Prayer to Overcome Negative Thinking

Dear Jesus,

Thank You for identifying strongholds in my mind that keep me from living to my full potential.

I confess that negative thinking has taken my mind hostage and kept me from living a life of faith that is free from shame, guilt, worry, and fear.

I have allowed outside voices and influences to take my thoughts captive and ignored the damage they have caused in my life and relationships.

Lord, I confess wrong thinking in the areas of (list areas below):

_____   _____
_____   _____
_____   _____

You tell us in 1 Peter 5:8 to be sober-minded and alert because our adversary the devil is prowling around like a roaring lion, looking for anyone to devour. I acknowledge he has caught me off guard and attacked my mind with negativity that I left unchecked.

Please forgive me for my apathy in guarding my heart and mind. I choose to be alert and sober minded as You renew and transform my thinking. In Jesus' name, I reject the lies of the enemy and stand on the Word of Truth. Amen.

Credit: https://praywithconfidence.com/prayer-for-negative-thoughts/

Declarations to Overcome Negative Thinking

I make my declaration known today to live victoriously over chronic negativity as a dominant influence in my life.

I choose to make winning over negativity an everyday habit.

Today, I declare that I shall put away the old ways in which I focused on and gave life to negative thinking, speaking, and living.

I put on a new garment, filled with thanksgiving, praise and hope.

I renounce all forms of negativity that seek to kill my hope and my ability to walk in believing faith.

I repent of and renounce all discouragement, depression, hopelessness, despair, doubt, unbelief, self-pity, victim thinking, self-loathing, criticism, suspicion, accusation, condemnation, and shame that keep me from living in God's hope.

I put away all unworthiness, all self-hatred, rejection, and other strongholds that keep me from walking with a greater revelation of my identity and my destiny in Christ.

In the place of negativity, I decide to feast only on the hope-filled nature of God in all things.

I set aside time to focus solely on the love, truth, promises and the goodness of God.

I kill all negative relationship patterns that keep me bound in ways that are toxic.

I choose not to deny problems, but to live from a place in God that is superior to those problems.

I declare today that I shall grow in thinking and speaking hope which involves focusing on God's goodness, what God is doing, His love, truth, the promises of God, the praises of God, encouragement to others, thanksgiving, and intimate worship.

I determine to:
- focus more on God's promises than on problems.
- speak with hope about even the toughest of issues.
- be solution focused rather than problem focused.

- refrain from reacting and giving voice to pessimism, criticism of others, self-criticism, and other forms of unbelief.
- remove gossip, slander and judgmentalism away from my conversations about others.
- speak about problems to the right people in the right way.
- cultivate thoughts, words and actions that increase hope and fruitfulness in the days to come.

Credit: https://markdejesus.com/declaration-for-overcoming-negativity/

Chapter Two

Overcoming Rape & Molestation: Breaking Free from the Victim Mentality

First John 5:4 says, *For everyone born of God is victorious and overcomes the world; and this is the victory that has conquered and overcome the world—our [continuing, persistent] faith [in Jesus the Son of God].*

I believe everything that has happened and will happen to me has an intended purpose, and I must discover that purpose. In my childhood, I was raped by one male and molested by five males, and one female. For more than half my life I walked around with a sign on my chest that said, *VICTIM*. I was in bondage to the emotional, physical, and spiritual scars that can come from being raped and molested at a young age. These scars made me a victim twice, once in my childhood and again in my adulthood, when I had to confront these sexual traumas.

The opposite of a victim is a victor. Merriam-Webster defines a victim as *one that is subjected to oppression, hardship, or mistreatment.* Merriam-Webster defines victor as *a person who defeats an enemy or opponent in a battle, game, or other competition*; so, it follows that victory is defined as an act of defeating an enemy or opponent in a battle, game, or other competition. First Corinthians 15:57 says, ... *but thanks be to God, who gives us the victory [as conquerors] through our Lord Jesus Christ.*

In 1988, my family and I moved from North Carolina to Temple Hills, Maryland. We lived in an apartment in Maryland off St. Barnabas Road behind a bowling alley. I was five years old when I was raped by a boy who was three years older than me. I don't recall the time of year the rape took place, but I can clearly remember that horrific day. My life would forever be changed. The events and incidents that followed created a crescendo of sexual trauma that reverberated into my adult years.

I lived with my mom, dad, and older brother. I often went outside with my brother and played with his friends' younger siblings. I don't recall if it was a school day, but I do remember it was warm enough for kids to be outside playing. All the neighborhood kids loved to get together and play a big game of hide-and-go-seek. When there were too many kids, we'd hide in pairs, so the game wouldn't be so hard and wouldn't go on forever. We had no method of choosing partners other than picking whoever was nearest to us. I just happened to be near a boy who was my brothers' friend and lived in my neighborhood. He was light-skinned with freckles, red hair, and thick red lips. He grabbed my arm, and we ran into the woods behind the apartments along with the other children and their partners to find a good hiding spot.

I remember his hand was sticky and damp with sweat. He ran with my forearm in his hand the whole time, basically pulling me along. We ran deep into the woods for a while because my legs were tired, my arm hurt from his grip, and the screams of the other children were distant. Finally, we stopped running and I rested against a nearby tree. I was tired but still caught up in the excitement of playing hide-and-go-seek, one of my favorite games to play. The thrill of wondering if I would be found or win the game was all I could think about. Usually when we would play I'd never win because I wasn't a good hider. This day, I believed that since we had run so far, we would win, but little did I know my partner had other plans for me. Thinking back, I believe his intentions were premeditated.

After I caught my breath, I asked myself where exactly we were supposed to be hiding, because it seemed like we were just standing behind trees, which wasn't a good hiding spot in my five-year-old opinion. I wasn't really paying attention to him, instead I was looking back. I don't remember what he was doing, but when I turned to see where he was, he was right in my face. He was standing so close to me. He put both hands on the tree around me and pressed himself into me, pressing me hard against the tree. I can still remember the cold hard tree against my back.

At this point, he was so close that his lips were almost touching mine and I could feel his hot breath on my face. He was breathing hard and slowly. I felt like I was going to suffocate from his weight and from the funk of his breath that smelled like old hotdogs and underarm pits. As I turned my face away to try and get some fresh air, he grabbed my face and tried to kiss me. I held my lips tightly together in disgust, but I felt his tongue trying to force its way into my mouth followed by teeth and saliva.

I can't recall what happened between the nasty kiss and what came next, but I do remember noticing that we were standing by a ravine that I hadn't noticed before. There was a slight drop with a stream of water at the bottom. I remember him standing behind me holding both my arms and saying in a low husky voice, "If you scream, I will throw you down there and the alligators will eat you." I felt his breath and his lips touch my right ear as he talked. I was terrified and all I could think about was the alligators eating me. I was paralyzed with fear. He said, "Do everything I say do." He was taller and bigger than me, so I agreed. Something inside of me said, *RUN*, but my legs would not work. All I could think about was the alligators. I did everything he said, and I didn't scream. He laid a jacket on the ground. To this day I don't remember either of us having a jacket on or where he got the jacket from. He told me to lay on the jacket on my stomach. I was scared so I did as I was told.

The ground was cool and hard. I remember hearing leaves crunching so maybe it was fall. I also recall the smell of dirt as I laid there. He straddled me from behind and began grinding himself against me. I felt like I couldn't breathe from his weight and at this point, the side of my face was in the dirt. I felt his breath on my neck and felt him lick and kiss the back of my neck a couple of times. After an immeasurable amount of time, I felt him stop; I didn't know then what he was doing, but I know now he was unbuttoning his pants because next, he pulled my pants and underwear down. I just remember laying there still, quiet and scared. I didn't know what was happening.

I was still lying flat on my stomach as he positioned himself, this time with our skin touching and his penis grinding against my bottom. I was unaware then, but now I know he wasn't quite sure what to do because it took him some time to figure it out, but once he was erect, he was able to penetrate me anally, at which point, I felt pressure, pain and then I blacked out. I don't know how long this act lasted or when it ended, but my memory picks back up as we were walking through the woods back home. There were no other kids around and it seemed late in the day because it was getting dark outside. He walked me back to the edge of the woods where he reminded me of what he would do to me (throw me in the ravine with the alligators) if I told anyone. He left me standing there and ran off to do whatever. I slowly walked back to my building where I was met by my mother, who was furious because she had been looking for me. It was around 6:00 p.m. when my dad got off work and because I was missing, she was late picking him up. I remember being scolded and shuffled into the car, so I never had a chance to tell my mom what happened. For years it was like having a red stain on a white shirt that constantly stayed in my memory. When I decided to write about it, the enemy tried to make me believe it didn't happen or that it was made up. But, the pain I remember was very real and the effects of the trauma were even more real. That day is so imprinted in my mind.

I can't remember how long we stayed in that apartment complex, but I do remember it wasn't long before we moved into a house. After the rape, I never remember seeing him ever again. Or, it could have been that I never went outside to play again. It was difficult to remember much after that day. I think the rape is the last memory I have of living at the apartment. I do have the memory of almost drowning at the complex's swimming pool. I remember the day I went missing when I tried to walk to my mother's friend's house, but I don't know if those instances came before or after the rape.

We moved to a house in Temple Hills. My mother would sometimes send my brother and I out of town to stay with relatives for spring break and sometimes a week of summer break. The molestations happened during this time and lasted over about four years between ages five and nine. I remember the ages because I recall the incidents started after the rape and continued until my little sister was born in 1992, when I was nine. That is also when my mom stopped sending us to North Carolina during school breaks. Although I can't remember the order when they occurred, I do remember the incidents well.

The first incident I remember was with my father's uncle. I recall my great uncle and I were sitting in a pickup truck in a field. He unzipped his pants and pulled his penis out. This is the first time I remember seeing an actual penis. I don't recall exactly how old I was. He wanted me to touch it. I didn't want to touch it. I thought I would hurt him if I touched it. He wasn't erect and since he was an old man, it looked weird just lying there, and I didn't want to touch it. I remember him grabbing my hand to guide me to touch him, but I kept pulling my hand back. He got upset and said I would get in trouble if I didn't touch it, so I touched it. He said, "See you're not hurting me." I just remember holding my hand on it. He said, "Rub it." So, I did, but nothing really happened. After I rubbed it, he put it away and we went back to the house. This was a one-time event. I never told anyone, and I don't remember feeling any emotion. However, I do remember wondering what other penises looked like. My father's uncle passed away when I was young.

On another occasion, I was molested by a female relative. She wanted to see what my breasts looked like, and she wanted to know if I had pubic hair. This happened as we were changing for bed. That night we both slept in the same bed. I remember her asking if I had ever kissed anyone. I said, "No." She suggested I try it with her. Again, I held my lips tight together because it was a nasty experience. After the kiss I am not sure exactly what happened next or how we got to where we did, but I was laying on my back and she was on top of me in the missionary position. She was trying to grind in between my legs. I remember lying there unsure of what was going on. After a little while, she stopped and lay next to me. She said, "Did that feel good?" I said, "No. I didn't feel anything." She sighed, rolled over, and went to sleep. I just laid there for a while. I don't remember going to sleep. I didn't say, "Stop!" I didn't scream for help. I just did what she told me to do, though I sensed it was wrong. I never told anyone about that either (although she never threatened me not to tell), and it never happened with her again.

I was later molested repeatedly by a male relative I refer to as the *primary molester*. Those dirty experiences included everything from touching my privates with clothes on and off, fingering, dry-humping, and me performing oral sex. This went on for years at so many different occasions. Sometimes it would happen multiple times a day, morning, noon, and night. These instances never included penetration. They were so frequent that I just expected it to happen and did what he asked of me. His favorite thing was touching my privates and then having me perform oral sex on him. He taught me how to *do it right*, not scrape him with my teeth, slow down, and focus. One time he invited one of his friends to touch me. He touched my breast and dry humped me for a little while before the *primary molester* stopped him. That same day, another friend of his came by, and the *primary molester* told me to go in the closet with his friend. He touched my privates, and I gave him a hand job. When we were done, he left me in the closet. I could hear them both in the room, but I was left in the closet for hours. They finally let me out before any adults came home.

Whenever I saw this male relative, he would touch me, or I would perform oral sex on him. That was the "norm." I grew used to it. He never threatened me, but he did say that it was "our little secret", and I couldn't tell anyone else about it or he would get in trouble. So, I never told anyone. For a long time, I felt guilty about it because I let it go on for so long, and I knew it wasn't right. I knew because he would always remind me that it was a secret. I never really felt anything during those times. I couldn't understand how he seemed to feel pleasure from something I felt nothing from.

The last molester from my childhood was my uncle's girlfriend's son. Like the others, he was older than me. My family and I had come for a visit and stayed with my uncle and his family. One night my uncle's girlfriend cooked spaghetti. I don't remember eating any. Everyone who ate some got food poisoning and had to go to the hospital. Her son, my drunk uncle, and I were left at the house while everyone else went to the hospital. My uncle was in bed. The son and I were in the living room watching TV. He wanted us to go into his room. We went into his room, and I sat on the bed. He asked if I wanted to see his penis. I was unsure, and I started to feel kind of afraid. I got up to go to the door. He got up, locked the door, and stood in front of it. He pressed me against the wall facing him. He told me to pull my pants down. It was dark in the room except for the light from a small lamp on the nightstand. I pulled my pants down, he also pulled his down. He came up to me, and I could see that his penis was curved. He tried to penetrate me while I was standing against the wall. His penis felt hard. I told him I didn't want to. He said it wouldn't hurt and it wouldn't take long. I was afraid, so I asked if we could do something else hoping he would stop trying to do whatever he was trying to do. He agreed. I was relieved until he threatened me. He said he would kill me if I told anyone. I pulled my pants up. He told me to go sit on the bed. I sat on the side of the bed as he laid down on the bed with his pants off. He asked me to put my mouth on his penis and he would let me go afterwards. He said I had to do it for at least one minute. There was a clock in the room, and I watched the clock as I performed oral sex on him. When one minute was up, I ran out of the room to the room I was staying in and never came back out for the rest of the night. For a couple days after that I had a dry ring around my mouth that was itchy and irritating. I remember feeling dumb afterwards. But, other than the first time when I was raped, with him was the only time I felt fear. I was afraid because I thought he would really hurt me if I didn't do what he said, and if he stuck his curved penis in me. He has been incarcerated for many years since then, though it is possible I was not his first victim. Prior to my uncle dating his mom, it was rumored that her daughter was removed from her custody due to allegations of rape and molestation. The only time I had experienced penetration was in my behind when I was raped the first time. I remembered that pain.

There was one other incident with him where he was caught by my mom with his hand on my private area. I was the only one who got in trouble. That was the last time I remember something happening with him. Sometimes, I think about what I could have done differently. *What if I had told someone as soon as it happened? What if I fought? What if I said, "No"?* For many years I carried a lot of guilt, shame, and embarrassment surrounding these sufferings I've just shared from my childhood. It was not easy sharing them, but I know they needed to be shared because I am not the only person who has experienced childhood sexual abuse (CSA).

****

I think it's important that I stop and talk about CSA, as a trained sexual assault victim advocate, I cannot pass up an opportunity to educate.

CSA is a significant public health problem and an adverse childhood experience (ACE). CSA refers to the involvement of a child (person less than 18 years old) in sexual activity that violates the laws or social taboos of society and that he/she:

- does not fully comprehend;
- does not consent to or is unable to give informed consent to, or
- is not developmentally prepared for and cannot give consent to.

Many children wait to report or never report child sexual abuse. Therefore, the numbers below likely underestimate the true impact of the problem. Although estimates vary across studies, the research shows:

- About 1 in 4 girls and 1 in 13 boys in the United States experience child sexual abuse.
- Someone known and trusted by the child or child's family members perpetrates 91% of child sexual abuse.
- The total lifetime economic burden of child sexual abuse in the United States in 2015 was estimated to be at least $9.3 billion.

Experiencing child sexual abuse can affect how a person thinks, acts, and feels over a lifetime. This can result in short-term and long-term physical, mental, and behavioral health consequences.

Examples of physical health consequences include:
- sexually transmitted infections (STIs)
- physical injuries
- chronic conditions later in life, such as heart disease, obesity, and cancer

Examples of mental health consequences include:
- depression
- posttraumatic stress disorder (PTSD) symptoms

Examples of behavioral consequences include:
- substance use/misuse, including opioid misuse.

- risky sexual behaviors, meaning sex with multiple partners or behaviors that could result in pregnancy or STIs.
- increased risk for perpetration of sexual violence.
- increased risk for suicide or suicide attempts

Experiencing child sexual abuse can also increase a person's risk for future victimization. For example, recent studies have found:
- Females exposed to child sexual abuse are at 2-13 times increased risk of sexual violence victimization in adulthood.
- People who experienced child sexual abuse are at twice the risk for non-sexual intimate partner violence.

Adults are responsible for ensuring that children have safe, stable, nurturing relationships and environments. Resources for CSA have mostly focused on treatment for victims and criminal justice-oriented approaches for perpetrators. These efforts are important after child sexual abuse has occurred. However, little investment has been made in primary prevention or preventing child sexual abuse. Effective evidence-based strategies are available to proactively protecting children from child sexual abuse, but few have been widely disseminated. More resources are needed to develop, evaluate, and implement evidence-based CSA primary prevention strategies. These strategies can help ensure that all children have safe, stable, nurturing relationships and environments.

Credit: https://www.cdc.gov/violenceprevention/childsexualabuse/fastfact.html

****

> All I could do was associate sex with pain.

I tried so many times to erase these memories from my mind and pretend like it didn't happen, and I was successful until high school when it seemed everyone was having sex. By this time, I had realized exactly what happened when I was raped, and if that was what sex was like I wanted no parts of it. All I could do was associate sex with pain. So, I decided I would never have sex, because I never wanted to experience pain like I'd experienced that day. I was terrified of sex and the thought of sex made me very uncomfortable. For years, I associated rape with sex until a close friend of mine clarified. What happened to me when I was raped was not sex, it was assault and abuse, and I shouldn't compare the two. That conversation was freeing and shifted my perspective.

The fear that fueled the victim mentality attached to what happened to me grew over the years. In my mind, I was a victim, and I would forever be a victim. We know 2 Timothy 1:7 says, *For God did not give us a spirit of timidity or cowardice or fear, but [He has given us a spirit] of power and of love and of sound a sound mind and personal discipline [abilities that result in a calm, well-balanced mind, and self-control].* Paul mentions three characteristics of a victor: power, love, and a sound mind. They are available to us because the Holy Spirit lives in us. All I needed to do was follow His leading each day so that my life would more fully exhibit these characteristics, but at the time I didn't know this yet.

While there is no formal psychological definition of a victim mentality, a useful, working definition is: looking at your entire life through a perspective in which things constantly happen *to* you. Victimization is thus a combination of seeing most things in life as negative, beyond your control, and as something you should be given sympathy for experiencing as though you *deserve* better. At its heart, a victim mentality is a way to avoid taking any responsibility for yourself or your life. By believing you have no power, then you don't have to act.

I made it through high school without sex and ventured off to college where I continued to abstain. In 2002, I moved back to Maryland from Pittsburgh and began talking to a guy I met on a college dating site. By this time, I felt, if I just *do it* then that will help me get over my fear. Well, God had other plans. I went to his house to watch a movie one night. He cooked dinner and after we ate, we began watching the movie. He was watching me more than he was watching the movie though. I was fully aware of him watching me and what was on his mind, so I just gave in. We started on the couch, then moved to his bedroom, where he asked if I looked at pornography. Yes, I watched pornography, but that was my dirty little secret, and I didn't want to watch it with someone else. We will discuss this dirty little secret and how to overcome lust in the next chapter.

Now, let me stop here and say, God will always give you a way out, and if you don't take it sometimes He will force a way. First Corinthians 10:13 says, *No temptation [regardless of its source] has overtaken or enticed you that is not common to human experience [nor is any temptation unusual or beyond human resistance]; but God is faithful [to His word—He is compassionate and trustworthy], and He will not let you be tempted beyond your ability [to resist], but along with the temptation He [has in the past and is now and] will [always] provide the way out as well, so that you will be able to endure it [without yielding, and will overcome temptation with joy].*

In a culture filled with moral depravity and sin-inducing pressures, Paul gave strong encouragement to the Corinthians about temptation. He said: (1) Wrong desires and temptations happen to everyone, so don't feel you've been singled out; (2) Others have resisted temptation, and so can you; (3) Any temptation can be resisted because God will help you resist it. God helps you resist temptation by helping you:

(a) recognize those people and situations that give you trouble (triggers); (b) run from anything you know is wrong; (c) choose to do only what is right; (d) pray for God's help; and (e) seek friends who love God and can offer help when you are tempted (accountability partners).

Running from a tempting situation is your first step on the way to victory (see 2 Timothy 2:22). God will always give you a way out or a way of escape, and in special cases, such as mine, He will force a way! Keep reading because my story is both sad and comical at the same time.

I declined watching the pornography, but this didn't stop other things from getting underway. After a couple of minutes in bed together, he got up to get a condom. When he came back, he asked me if I was ready. Before I could give him an answer, I caught a cramp in both legs, not just regular cramps, but it felt like both my legs turned into painful logs. This brought a halt to everything! I knew this was God forcing my way of escape. God is funny like that. If I'd given in to temptation, my entire testimony would have been different, and I wouldn't be writing this book. God knew the lives that would be saved and affected by my story. But that would've been completely nullified if I had sex that night!

Let's talk about sex for a moment. Sex is not a sin, but sex outside of marriage is. There are consequences that surpass the passing pleasure that illicit sex affords. The Bible is filled with warnings about sex outside of marriage. Not only warnings but the reasons behind the warnings as well. The only thing people seem to know that God said about sex is, "Don't do it." And that's too bad because God is not against sex.

> God is pro-sex. Everything He created is good including sex.

After all, He created it. God is pro-sex. Everything He created is good including sex. And, seeing how He is the Creator we can safely assume that He knows infinitely more about the subject than anyone else. As the inventor of this marvelous gift, He knows how it works best. He knows how we can receive the maximum joy and benefit from sex. He also knows the potential pitfalls. But we don't like boundaries. So, we test the limits; we climb the fences; we charge past the warning signs. And ultimately, we face unnecessary consequences. Our tendency is to ignore Him and make decisions based on our inclinations or what we've heard or experienced. We are prone to adopt the world's philosophy about sex, a philosophy that looks good on paper but in the end collapses. It does not work.

God has a positive attitude about sex, but man has perverted sex. This perversion is what has led to pornography, masturbation, rape, molestation, child sex abuse, and sex trafficking. Sex trafficking is a type of human trafficking and is defined by the Trafficking Victims Protection Act of 2000[1] as, "the recruitment, harboring, transportation, provision, obtaining, patronizing, or soliciting of a person for the purpose of a commercial sex act."

> Anything can be perverted.

Webster's Dictionary defines perversion as *a diverting from the true intent or purpose; a change to something worse; a turning or applying to a wrong end or use.* Anything can be perverted. Using opiates for non-medicinal purposes, for example, is a perversion of the poppy plant. In the Bible, the word translated *perversion* is used to define a deviation from righteousness in sexual behavior (see Leviticus 18:23; Romans 1:27; Ephesians 4:19; and Colossians 3:5), speech (see Proverbs 10:31), or justice (see Ecclesiastes 5:8). In each case, there are warnings against using for evil something that God created as good.

Satan twists things. Every good thing that God created, Satan works to pervert. God created sexuality and called it good (see Genesis 1:27-28, and 31). Sexual union has a dual purpose—procreation (see Genesis 1:28; and 9:1) and joining marriage partners as *one flesh* (see Genesis 2:24; Mark 10:8; and 1 Corinthians 6:16). Since early days, human beings have found

---

[1] https://www.congress.gov/bill/106th-congress/house-bill/3244

twisted uses for sex that accomplish neither of God's intended purposes. The perversions were so widespread by the time God gave the Law to Moses that admonitions against specific perversions had to be included in detail (see Leviticus 18:23; 20:12–13; and Deuteronomy 27:20). According to Scripture, any sexual activity outside the marriage union of one woman and one man is a perversion and condemned by God (see 1 Corinthians 6:18; Hebrews 13:4; and 1 Thessalonians 4:3). The New Testament lists some specific sexual perversions such as homosexuality, adultery, and fornication, stating that those who practice such aberrant behaviors *will not inherit the kingdom of God* (see 1 Corinthians 6:9–10; and Galatians 5:19–21).

> It is Satan who introduced the idea that perversion equals freedom.

Satan cannot create; that power belongs to God alone. So, he perverts what God has created. If he can entice God's most cherished creations to follow him in his twisted ideas, he succeeds in perverting the image of God we were designed to magnify (see 1 Corinthians 11:7). It is Satan who introduced the idea that perversion equals freedom. But he knows quite well that perversion is a slippery path that leads to bondage and then death (see Romans 2:5–8; and 2 Peter 2:19). By perverting sexuality, we mar the likeness of God in our own lives. But by using God's gifts in the way He intended them to be used, we find true freedom and can enjoy a healthy relationship with God (see Psalm 24:3–4; Matthew 5:8; and Galatians 5:1).

God's very first command to humankind in Genesis 1:28 was regarding sex. And, it was not, "don't do it." It was the very opposite, *Be fruitful and multiply.* God commanded Adam and Eve to get busy! Further evidence of God's positive attitude toward sex is revealed in the Song of Solomon. This book of the Bible is so descriptive that Hebrew boys were not allowed to read it until they were a certain age.

We need to understand that He is the Creator, and thus He is for sex. He is for great sex. At the same time, He is for us and our well-being. As our Heavenly Parent as well as our Creator, He has set up guidelines so that we can enjoy His gift to its fullest. The parameters are for our good, not our misery. That night I went to the guy's house, I mentioned earlier, I was trying to operate outside of God's guidelines and parameters to prove a point to myself. He is not out to deny us anything that is good for us. But even good things must be dealt with according to the Word of God.

Psalm 84:11 says, *For the Lord God is a sun and shield; The Lord bestows grace and favor and honor; No good thing will He withhold from those who walk uprightly.* God does not promise to give us everything we think is good, but He will not withhold what is permanently good. He will give us the means to walk along His paths, but we must do the walking. When we obey Him, He will not withhold anything back that will help us serve Him.

We have established that sex is good. Although sex is good, sex outside of marriage is out of order; and me having sex that night would not have helped me serve Him, nor would it have helped me overcome rape and molestation. So, I hobbled out of that apartment flustered and thankful that God caused the cramps and allowed my virginity to be maintained, but I still had the fear of sex as a result of my past trauma, and I knew it needed to be addressed.

Around this same time, I had enrolled in community college, so I could continue earning my Bachelor of Science Degree in Psychology. During one of my classes the professor had us journaling about our deepest darkest secrets, so we would know how our clients would feel sharing their secrets with someone. One day, when I left for work, I left my journal on the computer table and my mother read it. Yes, you guessed it. Two of the things I'd written about were the rape and molestations.

I came home from work to a hurt, confused, and concerned mother. I was 20 years old at the time, and still young and naïve. I felt like I was protecting my mother from finding out something she probably couldn't handle, but my secret was now out, and I had to talk about it with her. She felt like she'd failed to protect me and that made me feel bad. Although it had been a secret for so long, talking about it with my mom was very therapeutic! My mom recommended that I seek counseling for the way I felt about sex. I agreed that I would get help, but it took me another nine years of living in fear to do so.

In 2012, on my 29th birthday, I went to a Christian therapist for a consultation. She was the first I had been to and although I was nervous, I told her a couple things I was dealing with, and she accepted me as a client. Over the course of a year, we worked together, and I came to understand many things about myself and God's plan for my life.

Being raped and molested defined me, how I viewed sex, relationships between men and women and constructed the victim mentality I lived by. I believe that was Satan's plan for those horrible acts, however, God's plan was a plan of protection. I was terrified to have sex; therefore, it was not something that I was focused on. This protected me through high school, college and into my adult years until I could understand and accept God's design for sex within

> Today, I am 40 years old, a virgin, and I am committed to waiting until marriage to have sex.

marriage. Today, I am 40 years old, a virgin, and I am committed to waiting until marriage to have sex. I do feel like a lot of healing has taken place in reference to how I view and think of sex, but it won't be until I have sex with my husband that complete healing and restoration takes place.

> When something is scary, it triggers the brain's fight or flight or freeze or fawn response . . .

Relationship specialist, Robyn E. Brickel, M.A., LMFT, talks about how sexual abuse may trigger strong negative emotions linked to sexual desire or behavior for trauma survivors. When something is scary, it triggers the brain's fight or flight or freeze or fawn response—specifically the amygdala (the section of your brain responsible for fear), which we can't consciously control to just be different—we must feel differently.

The fight (facing any perceived threat aggressively) or flight (running away from the danger) or freeze (unable to move or act against a threat) or fawn (immediately acting to try to please to avoid any conflict) response is triggered by psychological or physical threats. It is a built-in defense mechanism implemented by evolution to cause physiological changes, including increased heart rate and heightened senses, enabling you to rapidly defend yourself from a perceived danger.

As we know from research, neurons that fire together wire together. This means fear and negative feelings can become triggered, automatically *hard wiring* to sexual responses because of past abuse. This is why trauma survivors often experience disgust, pain, discomfort during sex, or terrifying flashbacks from the past—even when they are safe with someone they choose in the present day.

A healthy sexual relationship—one based on love, compassion, caring, and in the context of marriage—is one place a trauma survivor can learn positive ways to experience sexual pleasure, desire, and consent. Healthy relationships for trauma survivors can be tremendous places to heal. I believe that is what God has in store for me.

Being raped at such a young age had a significant impact on my life but these horrible incidents also had a purpose. Today I have the honor of being able to share my story with people like you! Maybe your story isn't like mine, or maybe you have a story that is worse, the fact is, that your story has an intended purpose, it happened for a reason! Coming into an understanding of why horrible things happen to us and understanding God's purpose and design for the things the enemy tries to use for evil will help you overcome those things. Even more, knowing that Christ already won the battle thereby making you victorious will help you as well.

This knowledge helped me overcome being raped and molested and walking around with the victim mentality.

I understand being raped and molested when I was younger only contributed to and enhanced my testimony. God knew it was going to happen before I was born, and He knew I'd bounce back to use what the enemy meant for evil, for good. At this point in my life, I can confidently say, that I would not change being raped. I overcame being raped and molested, and I am free from the bondage of the victim mentality. The Bible says in 1 John 4:4, *Little children (believers, dear ones), you are of God, and you belong to Him and have [already] overcome them [the agents of the antichrist]; because He who is in you is greater than he (Satan) who is in the world [of sinful mankind].* It is easy to be overwhelmed by the problems we face. Evil is obviously much stronger than we are. John assures us, however, that God is even stronger. He will conquer all evil.

> At this point in my life, I can confidently say, that I would not change being raped.

Being raped and molested was very hard for me to endure, especially at a young age, and I did have moments where I asked, *Why me?* For years these memories scared me to my core in ways no other experiences have in my life. I dare not decrease the impact, but I want to emphasize the fact that God heals and delivers.

God Heals—Psalm 147:3 says, *He heals the brokenhearted and binds up their wounds [healing their pain and comforting their sorrow].*

God Delivers—Psalm 34:19 says, *Many hardships and perplexing circumstances confront the righteous, But the Lord delivers him from them all.*

God created you. He knows you. He is more acquainted with you than you are with yourself! If you have been raped, abused, or molested, you are built to overcome these things. Be encouraged that bad things don't happen to defeat you or take you out. I believe that they happen because they were intended to show you that you are strong enough to recover from these things and grow to a place where you can help those who are not strong enough yet to do the same. When the hits come, hit back, and remind yourself that everything that happens to you has an intended purpose. The things we experience in life are often allowed and even intended, not for our benefit but to inspire, encourage and affect others.

Now, the reality is, there are things in our past that just cannot be changed. But the way we view even the most painful things can be seen as a blessing when we view them through the lens of the Gospel. We can look back and see how God has sustained us and how we can now come alongside others in the moments of suffering that we share. By God's grace, we can be *comforted comforters*.

Second Corinthians 1:3-5 says, *³Blessed [gratefully praised and adored] be the God and Father of our Lord Jesus Christ, the Father of mercies and the God of all comfort, ⁴who comforts and encourages us in every trouble so that we will be able to comfort and encourage those who are in any kind of trouble, with the comfort with which we ourselves are comforted by God. ⁵For just as Christ's sufferings are ours in abundance [as they overflow to His followers], so also our comfort [our reassurance, our encouragement, our consolation] is abundant through Christ [it is truly more than enough to endure what we must].*

> The more we suffer, the more comfort God gives us.

Many think that when God comforts us, our troubles should go away. But if that were always so, people would turn to God only out of a desire to be relived of pain and not out of love for Him. We must understand that being comforted can also mean receiving strength, encouragement, and hope to deal with our troubles. The more we suffer, the more comfort God gives us. If you are feeling overwhelmed, allow God to comfort you. Remember, every trial you endure will help you comfort other people who are suffering similar troubles.

Over 2,000 years ago Jesus died, was buried, and resurrected. In this act of sacrificial love and obedience, Jesus was victorious over Satan. Christ's victory over the powers of darkness is our victory! Although my story is one of rape and molestation, that may not be your story. God does not allow rape, molestation, abuse, or any other terrible thing you may have experienced in your life to happen because He wanted you to be weak or have a victim mentality the rest of your life. He allowed it because He knew you could survive it and help others who need to hear your testimony to overcome and break free from the victim mentality!

Steps to Overcome a Victim Mentality
1. Ask God to reveal it to you (see Psalm 139:23-24).
2. Pray for God to change you (see John 15:5).
3. Be compassionate and tender-hearted (see Ephesians 4:31-32).
4. Set your mind on things above (see Colossians 3:1-2).

Credit: https://www.womendevotions.com/overcoming-a-victim-mentality/

A Prayer to Overcome a Victim Mentality

Father God, I choose to forgive those who used me, hurt me, abused, victimized, and traumatized me physically, sexually, mentally, or spiritually, or bullied me in any way. I forgive (Use the space below to name them, if able.)

_____   _____

_____   _____

_____   _____

I tear up the note against them, let them go free, and give them to the Lord for Him to deal with them. I receive the Lord's forgiveness for all unforgiveness towards others.

Today, I choose life when I've wanted to die many times. Today, I choose life to serve You and to be obedient to Your Word.

I repent for not allowing myself to be vulnerable and for not asking for help as I saw it as a weakness. I acknowledge I do need help, particularly Your help Jesus, because I cannot do things in my own strength.

I repent for allowing the enemy to keep me down. I repent of all self-belief of unworthiness, and not believing I deserved better. I repent for allowing this abuse to continue to receive attention.

I bind the victimization spirits, predator spirit, poverty spirit, self-pity spirit, rejection, self-hatred, dishonor, false pride, jealousy, unforgiveness, spiritual oppression, unclean spirits, emotional pain, spiritual pain, anxiety, stress, fear, despair, guilt, shame, helplessness, denial, agony, worthlessness, damaged goods mindset, and distrust. I break its power and send it to dry places. Father God, I break all ungodly soul tie attachments from myself to all abusers and command the abuser, independent and victim spirits, as well as all demon soul ties to go to the dry places, now in the strong name of Jesus Christ. I break all default programming of negative thinking, wrong thinking, or wrong mindsets, and choose to put on the mind of Christ and believe the Word over all negative words spoken over me that were not of love. I do deserve to be treated with respect, honor, and in high regard as a human.

I declare I am no longer a victim nor a target for abuse. In the strong name of Jesus Christ, I declare I can do all things through Christ who strengthens me. I choose today to see myself as a Child of the King. I receive, since I am bought with a price, that I am a royal priesthood and can walk with my head up high knowing I do deserve good things from God. I choose to accept the best from the Lord and not take the least ever again. In Jesus Name, I pray, Amen.

Declarations to Overcome a Victim Mentality:
I am a child of God (see John 1:12).
I am Jesus' friend (see John 15:15).

I am no longer a slave, but a son/daughter (see Galatians 4:5-7).

I have been adopted as a son/daughter (see Romans 8:15; Ephesians 1:5).

I am a son/daughter of God, and He is my Father (see Romans 8:14-15; Galatians 3:26; and 4:6).

I am an heir of God—a joint heir with Christ, sharing His inheritance with Him (see Galatians 4:6-7; and Romans 8:17).

I am united with the Lord and am one in spirit with Him (see 1 Corinthians 6:17).

I am saved by grace through faith and not of my works—I have nothing to boast about before God (see Ephesians 2:8-9).

I have peace with God and am reconciled to Him (see 2 Corinthians 5:18-19).

I am loved by Jesus and freed from my sins by His blood (see Revelation 1:5).

I have been forgiven of all my sins (see Colossians 2:13).

I have been washed, sanctified, and justified in the name of Jesus by the Holy Spirit (see 1 Corinthians 6:11).

I am a slave of God and a slave to righteousness (see Romans 6:18-19, and 22).

I am a fellow citizen with the rest of God's family (see Ephesians 2:19).

I am a partaker of Christ; I share in His life (see Hebrews 3:14).

I am one of God's living stones, being built up in Christ as a spiritual house (see 1 Peter 2:5).

I have been bought with a price and I belong to God (see 1 Corinthians 6:20).

I am dead to sin and alive to God (see Romans 6:11).

I am a new creation—the old is gone, the new has come (see 2 Corinthians 5:17).

I am a saint (see 1 Corinthians 1:2; Ephesians 1:1; Philippians 1:1; and Colossians 1:2).

I am righteous and holy (see Ephesians 4:24).

I have been justified (see Romans 5:1).

I have direct access to God through the Holy Spirit (see Ephesians 2:18).

I have been redeemed and forgiven of all my sins (see Colossians 1:14).

I am complete in Christ and have all I need (see Colossians 2:10).

I am free forever from condemnation (see Romans 8:1-2).

I am never left alone or forsaken (see Hebrews 13:5).

I am hidden with Christ in God (see Colossians 3:3).

I have been established, anointed, and sealed by God (see 2 Corinthians 1:21-22).

I have been delivered from the domain of darkness and transferred into the Kingdom of Jesus (see Colossians 1:13).

God's divine power has given me everything I need for a godly life (see 2 Peter 1:3).

I can resist the devil and he will flee from me (see James 4:7).

God has given me spiritual weapons and spiritual armor that are mighty through God to destroy enemy strongholds (see Ephesians 6:12-18; and 2 Corinthians 10:4-5).

I am strong in the Lord and in the strength of His might (see Ephesians 6:10).

I can stand firm against every scheme of the devil (see Ephesians 6:11).

I have victory through Christ (see 1 Corinthians 15:57).

I am more than a conqueror—overwhelming victory is mine in Jesus (see Romans 8:37).

I have overcome the world (see 1 John 5:4).

I overcome the enemy by the Blood of the Lamb and the words of my testimony (see Revelation 12:11).

Greater is He who is in me than he who is in the world (see 1 John 4:4).

I have not been given a spirit of fear, but of power, love and self-discipline (see 2 Timothy 1:7).

I am born of God and the evil one cannot touch me (see 1 John 5:18).

My name is written in Heaven & I have authority to trample over every power of the enemy so that nothing shall hurt me (see Luke 10:19-20).

I can find grace and mercy in my time of need, coming before God with confidence (see Hebrews 4:16).

I am assured that all things work together for my good (see Romans 8:28).

I am free from any condemning charges against me because God is for me (see Romans 8:31-34).

I am constantly being prayed for according to the perfect will of God by Jesus (see Romans 8:34; and Hebrew 7:25).

I cannot be separated from the love of God that is in Jesus (see Romans 8:35-39).

I can do all things through Christ who strengthens me (see Philippians 4:13).

I am confident that the good work God has started in me He will see through to completion (see Philippians 1:6).

I am a minister of reconciliation for God (see 2 Corinthians 5:17-21).

I am the salt of the earth (see Matthew 5:13).

I am the light of the world (see Matthew 5:14).

I am chosen by God, holy and dearly loved (see Colossians 3:12; and 1 Thessalonians 1:4).

I am a member of Christ's Body and have a unique role to play in the Church (see 1 Corinthians 12:27; and Ephesians 5:30).

I am seated in the Heavenly places with Jesus (see Ephesians 2:6)

I am a temple—a dwelling place of God. His Spirit and His life dwells in me (see 1 Corinthians 6:19).

I am God's co-worker (see 1 Corinthians 3:9; and 2 Corinthians 6:1)

I have been purchased with the imperishable and precious blood of Jesus (see 1 Peter 1:19).

I can approach God with freedom, confidence, and boldness through Jesus (see Ephesians 3:12; and Hebrews 4:16).

I am a child of light, not of darkness (see 1 Thessalonians 5:5).

I am a member of a chosen race, a royal priesthood, a holy nation, God's special possession (see 1 Peter 2:9-10).

I have been chosen and appointed to bear fruit, fruit that will last (see John 15:16).

I have received all of God's promises in Jesus Christ (see 2 Corinthians 1:20).

I am God's workmanship, created to do good works (see Ephesians 2:10).

I am a partaker of God's divine nature (see 2 Peter 1:4).

I was chosen by God before the creation of the world (see Ephesians 1:4).

I am an expression of the life of Christ because He is my life (see Colossians 3:4).

I am a holy partaker in a Heavenly calling (see Hebrews 3:1).

I am a branch of the true vine, a channel of His life to others (see John 15:1, 5).

<small>Credit: Adapted from Rodney Hogue, Liberated & Neil Anderson, Living Free in Christ</small>

Chapter Three

Overcoming Lust: Breaking Free from the Cycle of Sin

Run away from youthful lusts—pursue righteousness, faith, love, and peace with those [believers] who call on the Lord out of a pure heart.
2 Timothy 2:22

Running away is sometimes considered cowardly. But wise people realize that removing themselves physically from temptation can often be the most courageous action to take. Timothy, a young man, was warned to flee anything that produced evil thoughts. Do you have recurring temptation that is difficult to resist? Remove yourself physically from any situation that stimulates your desire to sin. Knowing when to run is as important in spiritual battle as knowing when and how to fight.

First Timothy 6:11-12 says, *[11]But as for you, O man of God, flee from these things; aim at and pursue righteousness [true goodness, moral conformity to the character of God], godliness [the fear of God], faith, love, steadfastness, and gentleness. [12]Fight the good fight of the faith [in the conflict with evil]; take hold of the eternal life to which you were called, and [for which] you made the good confession [of faith] in the presence of many witnesses.*

Active verb is the term used to indicate an action, process or sensation as opposed to a state of being or passivity. Paul uses active and forceful verbs to describe the Christian life: flee, pursue, fight, take hold. Some think Christianity is a passive religion that advocates waiting for God to act. But we must have active faith, obeying God with courage and doing what we know is right.

James 2:14-26 says, *[14]What is the benefit, my fellow believers, if someone claims to have faith but has no [good] works [as evidence]? Can that [kind of] faith save him? [No, a mere claim of faith is not sufficient—genuine faith produces good works.] [15]If a brother or sister is without [adequate] clothing and lacks [enough] food for each day, [16]and one of you says to them, "Go in peace [with my blessing], [keep] warm and feed yourselves," but he does not give them the necessities for the body, what good does that do? [17]So too, faith, if it does not have works [to back it up], is by itself dead [inoperative and ineffective].*

[18]But someone may say, "You [claim to] have faith and I have [good] works; show me your [alleged] faith without the works [if you can], and I will show you my faith by my works [that is, by what I do]." [19]You believe that God is one; you do well [to believe that]. The demons also believe [that], and shudder and bristle [in awe-filled terror—they have seen His wrath]! [20]But are you willing to recognize, you foolish [spiritually shallow] person, that faith without [good] works is useless? [21]Was our father Abraham not [shown to be] justified by works [of obedience

which expressed his faith] when he offered Isaac his son on the altar [as a sacrifice to God]? ²²You see that [his] faith was working together with his works, and as a result of the works, his faith was completed [reaching its maturity when he expressed his faith through obedience].

²³And the Scripture was fulfilled which says, "Abraham believed God, and this [faith] was credited to him [by God] as righteousness and as conformity to His will," and he was called the friend of God. ²⁴You see that a man (believer) is justified by works and not by faith alone [that is, by acts of obedience a born-again believer reveals his faith]. ²⁵In the same way, was Rahab the prostitute not justified by works too, when she received the [Hebrew] spies as guests and protected them, and sent them away [to escape] by a different route? ²⁶For just as the [human] body without the spirit is dead, so faith without works [of obedience] is also dead.

> True faith transforms our conduct as well as our thoughts.

When someone claims to have faith, what he or she may have is intellectual assent—agreement with a set of Christian teachings—and as such it would be incomplete faith. True faith transforms our conduct as well as our thoughts. If our lives stay unchanged, we don't truly believe the truths we claim to believe. We cannot earn our salvation by serving and obeying God. But such actions show that our commitment to God is real. Works of loving service are not a substitute for, but rather a verification of, our faith in Christ.

At first glance, James 2:18, seems to contradict Romans 3:28 which says, *For we maintain that an individual is justified by faith distinctly apart from works of the Law [the observance of which has nothing to do with justification, that is, being declared free of the guilt of sin and made acceptable to God].* Deeper investigation, however, shows that the teachings of James and Paul are not at odds. While it is true that our good works can never earn salvation, true faith always results in a changed life and good works. Paul speaks against those who try to be saved by works instead of true faith. James speaks against those who confuse mere intellectual assent with true faith. After all, even demons know who Jesus is, but they don't obey Him. True faith involves a commitment of your whole self to God.

James says that Abraham was considered "righteous" for what he *did*. Paul says he was justified *because* he believed God (see Romans 4:1-5). Again, James and Paul are not contradicting but complementing each other. Let's not conclude that the truth is a blending of these two statements. We are not justified by what we *do* in any way. True faith always results in works, but the works alone do not justify us. Faith brings us salvation; active obedience demonstrates that our faith is genuine.

Chapter Three: Lust

Lust is a very real sin, not only among unbelievers but for believers as well. The Oxford Dictionary defines lust as a very strong sexual desire; a passionate desire for something or a sensual appetite regarded as sinful. The Bible defines lust as something that is very different from love. Lust is selfish, and when we give in to it, we do so with little regard for the consequences. Lust is a harmful distraction that pulls us away from God. It is important that we gain control of it and pursue instead the type of love that God desires for us.

Again, lust is a sin, and the Bible describes lust as sinful, a form of faithlessness and immorality that *comes not from the Father but from the world.* Believers are warned to guard against it. Jesus teaches about lust in Matthew 5:27-30, which says, *27"You have heard that it was said, 'You shall not commit adultery'; 28but I say to you that everyone who [so much as] looks at a woman with lust for her has already committed adultery with her in his heart. 29If your right eye makes you stumble and leads you to sin, tear it out and throw it away [that is, remove yourself from the source of temptation]; for it is better for you to lose one of the parts of your body, than for your whole body to be thrown into hell. 30If your right hand makes you stumble and leads you to sin, cut it off and throw it away [that is, remove yourself from the source of temptation]; for it is better for you to lose one of the parts of your body than for your whole body to go into hell.*

> To be faithful to your spouse with your body but not your mind is to break the trust so vital to a strong marriage.

The Old Testament law said that it is wrong for a person to have sex with someone other than his or her spouse (see Exodus 20:14). But Jesus said the *desire* to have sex with someone other than your spouse is mental adultery and thus sin. Jesus emphasized that if the *act* is wrong, then so is the *intention*. To be faithful to your spouse with your body but not your mind is to break the trust so vital to a strong marriage. Jesus is not condemning natural interest in the opposite sex or even healthy sexual desire, but the deliberate and repeated filling of one's mind with fantasies that would be evil if acted out.

When Jesus said get rid of your hand or your eye He was speaking figuratively. He didn't mean literally to gouge out your eye, because even a blind person can lust. But if that were the only choice, it would be better to go to Heaven with one eye or hand than to go to hell with two. We sometimes tolerate sins in our lives that, left unchecked, could eventually destroy us. It is better to experience the pain of removal (getting rid of a bad habit or something we treasure, for instance) than to allow the sin to bring judgement and condemnation. Examine your life for anything that causes you to sin and take necessary action to remove it swiftly.

Mark 7:20-23 says, *²⁰And He said, "Whatever comes from [the heart of] a man, that is what defiles and dishonors him. ²¹For from within, [that is] out the heart of men, come base and malevolent thoughts and schemes, acts of sexual immorality, thefts, murders, adulteries, ²²acts of greed and covetousness, wickedness, deceit, unrestrained conduct, envy and jealousy, slander and profanity, arrogance and self-righteousness and foolishness (poor judgment). ²³All these evil things [schemes and desires] come from within and defile and dishonor the man."*

An evil action begins with a single thought. Allowing our minds to dwell on lust, envy, hatred, or revenge will lead to sin. Don't defile yourself by focusing on evil. Instead, we need to follow Paul's advice in Philippians 4:8:

Finally, believers, whatever is true, whatever is honorable and worthy of respect, whatever is right and confirmed by God's word, whatever is pure and wholesome, whatever is lovely and brings peace, whatever is admirable and of good repute; if there is any excellence, if there is anything worthy of praise, think continually on these things [center your mind on them, and implant them in your heart].

> Above all, read God's Word and pray.

What we put into our minds decides what comes out in our words and actions. Paul tells us to program our minds with thoughts that are true, honorable, right, pure, lovely, of good repute, excellent, and praiseworthy. Do you have problems with impure thoughts or daydreams? Examine what you are putting into your mind through television, books, conversations, movies, magazines, music, social media, and online searches. Replace harmful input with wholesome material. Above all, read God's Word and pray. Ask God to help you focus your mind on what is good and pure. It takes practice, but it can be done.

Lust, along with so many other sins that grieved (or quenched) the Holy Spirit, held me in a cycle of sin for many years. When the word *quench* is used in Scripture, it is speaking of a suppressing fire. When believers put on the shield of faith, as part of their armor of God (see Ephesians 6:16), they are extinguishing the power of the fiery darts from Satan. Christ described hell as a place where the fire would not be *quenched* (see Mark 9:44, 46, and 48). Likewise, the Holy Spirit is a fire dwelling in each believer. He wants to express Himself in our actions and attitudes. When believers do not allow the Spirit to be seen in our actions or we do what we know is wrong, we suppress or quench the Spirit (see 1 Thessalonians 5:19). We do not allow the Spirit to reveal Himself the way that He wants to.

To understand what it means to grieve the Spirit, we must first understand that this shows the Spirit has personality.

Only a person can be grieved; therefore, the Spirit must be a divine person in order to have this emotion. Once we understand this, we can better understand how He is grieved, mainly because we too are grieved. Ephesians 4:30 tells us that we should not grieve the Spirit. Several Scriptures in Ephesians tell us we grieve the Spirit by living like the pagans (4:17-19), by lying (4:25), by being angry (4:26-27), by stealing (4:28), by cursing (4:29), by being bitter (4:31), by being unforgiving (4:32), and by being sexually immoral (5:3-5). To grieve the Spirit is to act out in a sinful manner, whether it is in thought only or in both thought and deed.

Both quenching and grieving the Spirit are similar in their effects. Both hinder a godly lifestyle. Both happen when a believer sins against God and follows his or her own worldly desires. The only correct road to follow is the road that leads the believer closer to God and purity, and farther away from the world and sin. Just as we do not like to be grieved, and just as we do not seek to quench what is good, so we should not grieve or quench the Holy Spirit by refusing to follow His leading.

It wasn't until I became sick of my sin and submitted fully to God that the Holy Spirit exposed my sins by shining the light of the Word on them. The Word of God showed me what God offers, which is so much better than what sin offers. God offers life and life more abundantly; sin only offers suffering, misery, and death.

I once read a post that said, *Sin fascinates, then it assassinates*. That post was so true and is a perfect example of lust, more specifically the lustful sins of masturbation and pornography. Masturbation and pornography are fascinating, they slowly draw you in, subtly with a picture or a touch that you deem as innocent, kind of like quicksand. The funny thing about quicksand is that you sink slowly, and you don't realize how deep you have gone until it's too late. Luckily, it's never too late for us because God loves us so much. It is not too late for you! I pray that what you read on these pages challenges you and encourages you to break the cycle of sin whether your struggle is with lust or with another sin. I want to focus for a moment on God's love for us by discussing two Scriptures, John 3:16 and Romans 2:3-4:

> Sin fascinates, then it assassinates.

John 3:16 (NIV) says, *For God so loved the world that he gave his one and only Son, that whoever believes in him shall not perish but have eternal life.* The entire gospel comes to focus on this verse. God's love is not static or self-centered; it reaches out and draws in. Here God sets the pattern of true love, the basis for all love relationships—when you love someone dearly, you are willing to give freely to the point of self-sacrifice. God paid dearly with the life of His Son, the highest price He could pay. Jesus accepted our punishment, paid the price for our sins, and then offered us the new life that He has bought for us. When we share the gospel with others, our love must be like Jesus'—willingly giving up our own comfort and security so that others might join us in receiving God's love. This is not an easy chapter to write, but it's worth it if you come to know and experience God's love.

> In eternal life there is no death, sickness, enemy, evil, or sin. When we don't know Christ, we make choices as though this life is all we have.

Some people are repulsed by the idea of eternal life because their lives are so miserable. But eternal life is not an extension of a person's miserable mortal life; eternal life is God's life embodied in Christ given to all believers now as a guarantee they will live forever. In eternal life there is no death, sickness, enemy, evil, or sin. When we don't know Christ, we make choices as though this life is all we have. This life is just the introduction to eternity. Receive this new life by faith and begin to evaluate all that happens from an eternal perspective. The ending of this Scripture says, ... *that whoever believes in Him shall not perish but have eternal life.* To believe is more than intellectual agreement that Jesus is God. It means to put our trust and confidence in Him that He alone can save us. It is to put Christ in charge of our present plans and eternal destiny. Believing is both trusting His words as reliable, and relying on Him for the power to change, turn away and flee from sin. If you have never trusted Christ, let this promise of everlasting life be yours today—and believe.

Romans 2:3-4 says, *³But do you think this, O man, when you judge and condemn those who practice such things, and yet do the same yourself, that you will escape God's judgment and elude His verdict? ⁴Or do you have no regard for the wealth of His kindness and tolerance and patience [in withholding His wrath]? Are you [actually] unaware or ignorant [of the fact] that God's kindness leads you to repentance [that is, to change your inner self, your old way of thinking—seek His purpose for your life]?* The New Testament is translated from the original Koine Greek language manuscripts. The word kind used here is the Greek word έρωμαι which means love, loving, or gracious. I have heard the end of this Scripture loosely quoted this way, *It's the love of God that draws men unto repentance.*

In His kindness (love and grace), God holds back His judgement, giving people time to repent. It is easy to mistake God's patience for approval of the wrong way we are living. Self-evaluation is difficult, and it is even more difficult to expose our conduct to God and let Him tell us where we need to change. But as Christians we must pray constantly that God will point out our sins, so that we can repent, turn from our sins, and heal. Unfortunately, we are more likely to be amazed at God's patience with others than humbled at His patience with us. Second Peter 3:9 says, *The Lord does not delay [as though He were unable to act] and is not slow about His promise, as some count slowness, but is [extraordinarily] patient toward you, not wishing for any to perish but for all to come to repentance.* To repent means to be convinced of another way, to change your mind or convictions. And in response be convinced in your mind and heart, to change your actions. Repentance means turning from going your own way to going God's way.

I struggled with the spirit of lust from age nine to age 39. My lustful sins of choice were masturbation and pornography. The first time I ever saw a naked picture, I was outside playing and came in the house for a drink of water. On the side of our house was the entrance to the garage, where we kept our trash cans. As I was going into the house, I saw a picture laying on top of the trash can. It was a close-up picture of a man and a woman having sex. I still remember standing there fascinated while looking at this picture. It seemed like I stood there for hours staring at the picture. At one point I even picked the picture up and held it in my hand to get a closer look at what was going on. This one picture planted a seed of sin and lust in me. I was curious now, and I had to know what was happening in this picture.

> Having a past that involved sexual trauma made me wonder how something that had caused me such pain seemed so enjoyable.

Thank God we didn't have a computer at the time, but my little mind was now in overdrive. I was too shy of a child to ask about sex, and somehow, I knew I shouldn't have been looking at the picture in the first place. One day I was looking in my older brother's closet for something and came across a pornographic VHS (I was a nosey child and was probably snooping, but I digress). I knew by the images on the cover that it was like the picture I'd seen. I couldn't watch it then, but I plotted on a time when I would be able to watch it. One day when I was home alone, I made a beeline to his closet, got that VHS, and watched the whole thing from beginning to end about three times. This only made the curiosity grow. Having a past that involved sexual trauma made me wonder how something that had caused me such pain seemed so enjoyable. I began to willingly and voluntarily water that seed that was planted with the photograph.

The first time I masturbated I was nine years old. I remember because it was just before my little sister was born. My mom was about eight months pregnant, and we had just

Chapter Three: Lust

experienced a house fire causing us to relocate. I will not go into the details of what I did, but it felt good for a couple seconds,

> I stayed in this sin so long because I felt it was the best I'd ever get. I settled for sin

literally only a few seconds. But something inside me was awakened that never should have been awakened at that age. Satan's bait had me hook, line, and sinker. The VHS was water for the seed, and now the seed had taken root. I wouldn't even realize the severity of my sins or that it was even a sin until years later. Throughout elementary, middle school, high school, and college, this was my dirty little secret, or so I thought. After I came to know and understand sex and masturbation, I knew flat out pornography was wrong, but I justified the masturbation by telling myself, "At least I am not having sex!" Oh, the lies we believe to justify our sins. To be completely open, honest, transparent, and vulnerable, because of the past sexual trauma I had experienced, I stayed in this sin so long because I felt it was the best I'd ever get. I settled for sin, even though I was never able to achieve an orgasm from masturbation or watching pornography. The only benefit I was reaping was death, and separation from God.

Let me stop here and say, Jesus Christ nullified every justification you could ever have to sin when He died on the Cross for our sins, therefore, there is no excuse. Jesus paid the cost of our sin so that we may be saved! Let me also say that there are no levels of sin. Those who lie are sinning against God just like those who are sleeping with multiple people or cheating on their spouse. These sins are the same in God's eyes. So, there are no justifications or severity levels when it comes to sin, however there is a difference in how the sins, we commit affect us spiritually. First Corinthians 6:18 says, *Run away from sexual immorality [in any form, whether thought or behavior, whether visual or written]. Every other sin that a man commits is outside the body, but the one who is sexually immoral sins against his own body.*

Christians are free to be all they can be for God, but they are not free from God. God created sex to be a beautiful and essential ingredient of marriage, but sexual sin—sex outside the marriage relationship including pornography (watching others have sex) and masturbation (self sex)—always hurts someone. It hurts God because it shows that we prefer following our own desires instead of the leading of the Holy Spirit. It hurts others because it violates the commitment necessary to a relationship. It often brings disease to our bodies. And it deeply affects our personalities, which respond in anguish when we harm ourselves physically and spiritually.

You see, all other sins a person commits are outside the body, except the sexually immoral; immoral, meaning a person, group, or situation that intentionally goes against accepted ideas of what is right; sins against one' own body. I was sinning against my own body, therefore sinning against God because my body is not my own. My body is a temple of the Most High. Watching porn and masturbating is a form of adultery. I was cheating on God and my future spouse.

First Corinthians 6:18 uses the word immoral, in the Greek immoral is translated as *Porneuo* meaning the one who continually prostitutes him or herself. I was prostituting myself to lust. For over 30 years I was being pimped by lust. That changes the perspective on things, doesn't it? Are you being pimped by lust? Pornography? Masturbation? Sexual immorality?

The origin of the word *pornography* reveals a great deal about its influence through the ages. It derives from the Greek word *pornographos* and simply means *the writing of prostitutes*. Originally, it described prostitutes and their trade, but later came to refer to writings and pictures intended to arouse sexual desire. Lewdness (the unlawful indulgence of lust, fornication, or adultery) is bitter and poisonous but enticing to those who are deceived by lust (see Ephesians 4:18-22). Nudity is a powerful enticement, as the sin of David and Bathsheba shows (see 2 Samuel 11:2-5). Adultery and fornication are born of lust and thrive on desire. The apostle James clearly expresses this process of entrapment in James 1:12-15, which says, *[12]Blessed [happy, spiritually prosperous, favored by God] is the man who is steadfast under trial and perseveres when tempted; for when he has passed the test and been approved, he will receive the [victor's] crown of life which the Lord has promised to those who love Him. ¹³Let no one say when he is tempted, "I am being tempted by God" [for temptation does not originate from God, but from our own flaws]; for God cannot be tempted by [what is] evil, and He Himself tempts no one. ¹⁴But each one is tempted when he is dragged away, enticed and baited [to commit sin] by his own [worldly] desire (lust, passion). ¹⁵Then when the illicit desire has conceived, it gives birth to sin; and when sin has run its course, it gives birth to death.*

The crown of life is like the victory wreath given to winning athletes. First Corinthians 9:25 says, *Now every athlete who [goes into training and] competes in the games is disciplined and exercises self-control in all things. They do it to win a [a]crown that withers, but we [do it to receive] an imperishable [crown that cannot wither].* At times we must even give up something we perceive as good to do what God wants. Each person's special duties determine the discipline and denial that he or she must accept. Without a goal, discipline is nothing but self-punishment. With the goal of pleasing God, our denial seems like nothing compared to the eternal, imperishable reward that will be ours.

The crown of life will be given to believers who persevere through temptations, tribulations, and persecutions. This crown is spoken of by Jesus as a reward for those who faithfully endure trials and attacks brought against them because of their uncompromising allegiance to Him and His Word. God's crown of life is not glory and honor here on earth, but the reward of eternal life—living with God forever. The way to be in God's winners' circle is by loving Him and staying faithful even under pressure.

Temptation comes from evil desires inside us, not from God. It begins with an evil thought and becomes sin when we dwell on the thought and allow it to become an action. Like a snowball rolling downhill, sin grows more destructive the more we let it have its way. The best time to stop temptation is before it is too strong or moving too fast to control.

> God *tests* people, but he does not *tempt* them by trying to seduce them into sin. God allows Satan to tempt people . . .

People who live for God often wonder why they still have temptations. Does God tempt them? God *tests* people, but he does not *tempt* them by trying to seduce them into sin. God allows Satan to tempt people, however, to refine their faith and help them grow in their dependance on Christ. We can resist the temptation to sin by turning to God for strength and choosing to obey His Word.

It is easy to blame others and make excuses for evil thoughts and wrong actions. We make excuses like:

"It's the other person's fault;"
"I couldn't help it;"
"Everybody's doing it;"
"It was a mistake;"
"Nobody's perfect;"
"The devil made me do it;"
"I was pressured into it;"
"I didn't know it was wrong;"
"God is tempting me."

A person who makes excuses is trying to shift the blame from himself or herself to something or someone else. A Christian, on the other hand, accepts responsibility for his or her wrongs, confesses them, and asks God for forgiveness.

Jesus also reveals that sexual perversions grow out of lust: Mark 7:21-23 says, *[21]For from within, [that is] out the heart of men, come base and malevolent thoughts and schemes, acts of sexual immorality, thefts, murders, adulteries, [22]acts of greed and covetousness, wickedness, deceit, unrestrained conduct, envy and jealousy, slander and profanity, arrogance and self-righteousness and foolishness (poor judgment). [23]All these evil things [schemes and desires] come from within and defile and dishonor the man.*

Pornography draws to the surface the desires simmering within. In a decadent society, those lusts bear the fruit of horrible sexual crimes like adultery, homosexuality, bestiality, rape, child molestation, and incest. Pornography degrades that which God created in His image (see Genesis 1:27). It brings man, created a little lower than the angels (see Psalm 8:5), down to the level of animals (see Jude 10). Lewdness is an insult to God; all that pornography glorifies and promotes is in direct and open violation of God's law. These are emphatically stated in Scripture: adultery (see Exodus 20:14; and Proverbs 6:32), carnal desire (see Ephesians 4:17-22; and Matthew 5:28), bestiality (see Deuteronomy 27:21; and Leviticus 18:23), incest (see Leviticus 18:6-9; and 20:11-14), rape (see Deuteronomy 22:25-27), sodomy (see Leviticus 18:22; Romans 1:26, and 27), child molestation (see Matthew 18:10).

Masturbation—there is more at work here than just a robotic act. It is a covetous desire which falls outside God's loving design. Masturbation is like a pressure cooker. Some pressure is released, but the water is still boiling. One man who was immersed in the sin of porn and masturbation says it's like gratifying himself to a corpse, using another person's image as a means to an end. But immersion in the practice becomes an endless cycle of tension, relief, shame, and guilt. There is no fulfillment in the act, unlike the one he gains from a godly and joyful marriage. Sex, as God designed it, is good, and it is meant to be an honest, relational act of love between a husband and his wife (one biological man and one biological woman). Those are the boundaries as set by the Lord. Masturbation is a selfish act that satisfies one's temporal, sinful desires.

The Bible does not specifically mention the word masturbation. The passage most often associated with masturbation is the story of Onan in Genesis 38:9–10. Some interpret this passage to say that *spilling your seed* is a sin. However, that is not what the passage is saying. God condemned Onan not for *spilling his seed* but because Onan was rebellious. Onan refused to fulfill his duty to provide an heir for his deceased brother. The passage is not about masturbation but about fulfilling a family obligation.

A second passage sometimes used as evidence that masturbation is a sin is Matthew 5:27–30. Jesus speaks against having lustful thoughts and then says, *If your right hand causes you to sin, cut it off and throw it away*. While there is clearly a connection between lustful thoughts and masturbation, it is unlikely that Jesus was alluding to the specific sin of masturbation in this passage. Interestingly enough, an older definition of masturbation is *self-abuse*. Although more

> an older definition of masturbation is *self-abuse*

modern dictionaries may no longer carry this definition, they are still linked together under self-abuse:

Self-abuse, noun
1. Abuse of oneself or one's abilities.
2. Masturbation.

First Corinthians 6:18 (NIV) further confirms this, saying that unlawful sexual relations defile our own bodies: *Flee from sexual immorality. All other sins a man commits are outside his body, but he who sins sexually sins against his own body.*

The Bible nowhere explicitly says that masturbation is a sin, yet there is no question the actions that usually lead to masturbation are sinful. Masturbation is nearly always the result of lustful thoughts, inappropriate sexual stimulation, and/or pornography. It is these problems that need to be dealt with. If the sins of lust, immoral thoughts, and pornography are forsaken and overcome, masturbation will become much less of an issue and temptation. Many people struggle with guilt concerning masturbation, when, in reality, they would be far better off repenting of the sins that lead them to masturbate.

As mentioned, the Bible does not directly address the issue of masturbation or deliberate self-stimulation of the sexual organ to the point of orgasm. It does warn against all forms of self-indulgence, adultery of the mind, and fornication. One of the problems involved is that though God created sex for enjoyment and pleasure, it is to be confined to the marriage relationship because it is also designed to express love (not just sexual love), unity, and total commitment. Masturbation is an act of self-gratification rather than a part of giving gratification and pleasure to one's partner.

Some Dangers of Masturbation:

1. **Psychic Effects.** Masturbation tends to isolate its captives psychologically and socially. In masturbation, the person is focused on self-alone though he or she usually is fantasizing about someone else at the same time.

2. **Emotional Deprivation.** It is impossible for the one who is practicing this habit to experience the full extent of sex emotions. Therefore, in short-circuiting the emotions one can easily be removed from the world of reality.

3. **Damaged Sensibility.** The habit of masturbation has a tendency in numbing the mechanism of the sexual organs if practiced excessively. This lessens the sensibility and thus detracts from normal sexual relations of married life.

4. **Self-Gratification.** The emotional background of self-gratification is not the least bit healthy and usually militates

against the home, wife, and family because it is focused only on self.

5. **Control of the Mind.** Along with the act of masturbation comes the fantasy of the mind. When practiced often, a pattern or cycle seems to become established within the individual's mind. Thus, perversion tends to control the mind and this in turn starts the act. The real danger lies in the guilt that increases as the individual dwells in this world of fantasy.

With that said, you may be asking yourself, *Isn't it still better to masturbate than to commit fornication?* The easy answer to this question would be, *Yes, it is better to masturbate, because at best it corrupts only one person. It certainly is the lesser of two evils.* However, why would a loving, holy, all-powerful God abandon you to a situation in which you must choose any evil, whether it be *lesser* or *greater*? To really answer this question, we must again go back to God's original plan for sex.

First of all, masturbation will not truly relieve the sexual pressure that one may feel. It may for a short moment, but in the long run it only creates a deeper desire and capacity for sex, which will lead to more masturbation. If you let yourself become enslaved to a sexual high, you will find that you need to go to increasingly extreme acts to maintain the same degree of excitement. There are even ungodly sex therapists who recommend masturbation as a way of increasing sexual desire, not lessening it. This creates a vicious circle, like the junkie who craves a *fix*, but is only temporarily satisfied. The more he indulges in his dependency, the more ensnared by addiction he becomes. This is the nature of all sin. That is why Jesus declared that all who sin become a slave to sin (see John 8:34).

Furthermore, masturbation usually involves fantasy, visualization, and often pornography. The Bible is very clear as to what God expects of us in these areas of fantasy and lust. It teaches that we must not look lustfully at each other, nor should we behave in such a manner as to entice others to lust after us. Job 31:1-3 (TLB) says, *¹I have made a covenant (agreement) with my eyes; How then could I gaze [lustfully] at a virgin? ²"For what is the portion I would have from God above, And what heritage from the Almighty on high? ³Does not tragedy fall [justly] on the unjust and disaster to those who work wickedness?* Job had not only avoided committing the great sin of adultery; he had not even taken the first step toward that sin by looking at a woman with lust. Job said he was innocent of both outward and inward sins. In chapter 29, Job reviewed his good deeds. Here in chapter 31, he listed sins he had not committed—in his heart (31:1-12), against his neighbors (31:12-33), or against God (31:24-34).

Chapter Three: Lust

> Sinful action is more dangerous than sinful desire, and that is why desires should not be acted out.

Matthew 5:28 says, *...but I say to you that everyone who [so much as] looks at a woman with lust for her has already committed adultery with her in his heart.* Some think that if lustful thoughts are sin, why shouldn't a person go ahead and do the lustful actions too? Acting out sinful desires is harmful in several ways: (1) It causes people to excuse sin rather than stop sinning; (2) it destroys marriages; (3) it is deliberate rebellion against God's Word; (4) it always hurts someone else in addition to the sinner. Sinful action is more dangerous than sinful desire, and that is why desires should not be acted out. Nevertheless, sinful desire is just as damaging to righteousness. Left unchecked, wrong desires will result in wrong actions and turn people away from God.

While the above verses refer to men lusting after women, all women know that it can very easily be reversed to apply to themselves as well. Men may be more easily visually stimulated than women, but women can be just as vulnerable to sexual fantasy in the emotional realm. Both are sin in God's eyes, and both can be brought into subjection by controlling our thoughts through Christ's power. All sexual immorality begins with a thought. A lustful thought not taken captive will eventually lead to other perversions, because sin reproduces itself in increasingly greater measures. If we do not deal with our evil thoughts, they will take root in our hearts. It is for this reason that God is so concerned with our thought life. Jesus came not only to deliver us from our "outward" sins, but also from wickedness that begins in the heart.

> People who are not satisfied with God's plan for sex commit idolatry by using evil things to experience weird and unlawful forms of sexual intercourse.

Since masturbation begins with sin in the mind, it might be called an *affair of the mind* because it brings about sexual sin inflicted against one's own body. Although it brings a short-lived gratification, it makes one feel defiled when continued on a regular basis. In fact, as we have discussed, it is a form of fornication because fornication is more than just sex with someone before marriage. It includes many other sexual sins such as pornography and the use of sexual toys for gratification. People who are not satisfied with God's plan for sex commit idolatry by using evil things to experience weird and unlawful forms of sexual intercourse. Some verses in Ezekiel actually describe this kind of fornication.

Ezekiel 16:15-17 says, *15But you trusted in and relied on your beauty and prostituted yourself [in idolatry and its debauched rituals] because of your fame, and you poured out your immoralities on every [willing] passer-by and your beauty was his [as you worshiped the idols of the Gentile nations].* ¹⁶*You took some of your clothes and made for yourself [decorated] high places and shrines of various colors and prostituted yourself on them—things which should never have come about and taken place.* ¹⁷*You also took your beautiful jewels and beautiful vessels made of My gold and My silver, which I had given you, and made for yourself images of men so that you could prostitute yourself with them; 18and you took your embroidered clothing and covered them and offered My oil and My incense before them.*

God cared for and loved Judah, only to have it turn away to other nations and their false God's. The nation grew to maturity and became famous, but they forgot who had given them their life (see Ezekiel 16:22). This is a picture of spiritual adultery called harlotry (turning from the one true God). As you become wise and more mature, don't allow pornography, masturbation, lust and/or sexual immorality to turn you away from the One who truly loves you.

Below you will find more biblical principles that can be applied to the issue:

Closed doors, pulled covers or darkness doesn't hide our deeds from God.

First Corinthians 10:31 says, *So then, whether you eat or drink or whatever you do, do all to the glory of [our great] God.* If we *cannot give God glory for something, we should not do it. God's love must so permeate our motives that all we do will be for His glory. Keep this as a guiding principle by asking, Is this action glorifying God? How can I honor God through this action?* or *Would I want God present while I was masturbating?* He already is present because He is Omnipresent (present everywhere at the same time). Closed doors, pulled covers or darkness doesn't hide our deeds from God.

Romans 14:23 says, *But he who is uncertain [about eating a particular thing] is condemned if he eats, because he is not acting from faith. Whatever is not from faith is sin [whatever is done with doubt is sinful].* If we are not fully convinced that an activity is honoring to God, it is a sin. We try to steer clear of actions forbidden by Scripture, of course, but sometimes Scripture is silent. Then, we should follow our consciences. *Whatever is not from faith is sin* means that to go against a conviction will leave a person with a guilty or uneasy conscience. When God shows us that something is wrong for us, we should avoid it. But we should not look down on other Christians who exercise their freedom in those areas.

Do you not know that your body is a temple of the Holy Spirit, who is in you, whom you have received from God? You are not your own; you were bought at a price. Therefore, honor God with your body (see 1 Corinthians 6:19–20). Our bodies have been redeemed and belong to God.

The fruit of the Spirit is . . . self-control (see Galatians 5:22–23). Masturbation is almost always a sign of a lack of self-control and self-discipline.

Do not gratify the desires of the flesh. For the flesh desires what is contrary to the Spirit, and the Spirit what is contrary to the flesh. They are in conflict with each other, so that you are not to do whatever you want... (see Galatians 5:16–17). We are called to self-denial, not to self-gratification. These truths should have a powerful impact on what we do with our bodies. Considering these principles, it is doubtful that masturbation could ever be a God-honoring activity. If masturbation could be done with:

- no lust in your heart;
- no immoral thoughts;
- no pornography;
- no self-gratification of the flesh;
- full assurance that it is good and right;
- thanks, given to God;

then perhaps it would be allowable. But those qualifiers seem to negate the very meaning and purpose of masturbation.

Lust is like a mosquito bite, the more you scratch it the more it itches. Sometimes though we know we shouldn't, we keep scratching because the scratching feels so good, not realizing that in the middle of our momentary pleasure, the scratching is causing damage to our skin or in the case of lust to the very fabric of our mind, body, soul, and spirit.

It is possible to gain control over lust. Lust is something almost all of us have experienced, and we live in a society that promotes it at every turn. However, the Bible is clear that believers should do everything they can to combat its control over them; see 1 Thessalonians 4:3-5, Colossians 3:5, 1 Peter 2:11 and Psalms 119:9-10. There are consequences of lust. When we lust, we bring several consequences into our lives. The Bible makes it clear that we're not meant to sustain ourselves on lust, but on love; see Galatians 5:19-21, 1 Corinthians 6:13 and Hebrews 13:4.

Let's talk about sin a little more in depth. Romans 6:23 says, *For the wages of sin is death, but the free gift of God [that is, His remarkable, overwhelming gift of grace to believers] is eternal life in Christ Jesus our Lord.* You are free to choose between two masters, but you are not free to manipulate the consequence of your choice. Each of the two masters pays with his own kind of currency. The currency of sin is death. That is all you can expect or hope for in life without God. Christ's currency is eternal life—new life with God that begins on earth and continues forever with God. What choice have you made?

Eternal life is a free gift from God. If it is a gift, then it is not something that we earn, nor something that must be paid back. Consider the foolishness of someone who receives a gift given out of love and then offers to pay for it. A gift cannot be bought by the recipient. A more appropriate response to a loved one who offers a gift is graceful acceptance with gratitude. Our salvation is a gift of God; not something of our own doing (see Ephesians 2:8-9). He saved us because of His mercy, not because of any righteous things that we have done (see Titus 3:5). How much more should we accept with thanksgiving the gift God has freely given to us.

At its core, sin is rebellion against God. Our sin separates us from God, who is the Creator and Sustainer of life. In John 14:6, Jesus said, *I am the [only] Way [to God] and the [real] Truth and the [real] Life; no one comes to the Father but through Me.* This is one of the most basic and important passages in Scripture. How can we know the way to God? Only through Jesus. Jesus is the way because He is both God and man. By uniting our lives with His, we are united with God. Trust Jesus to take you to the Father, and all the benefits of being God's child will be yours. Trusting Jesus means turning away from sin.

Jesus says He is the only way to God the Father. Some people may argue that this way is too narrow. It is wide enough for the whole world, if the world chooses to accept it. Instead of worrying about how limited it sounds to only have one way, we should be saying, *Thank You, God, for providing a sure way to get to You!* As the way, Jesus is our path to the Father. As the truth, He is the reality of all God's promises. As the life, He joins His divine life to ours, both now and eternally.

God is known as the great *I AM*. Life is in God. So, when we sin and become separated from God, we become separated from true life. Therefore, perforce (unavoidably or inevitability), we experience death.

Three points of clarification are needed:

First, sin does not necessarily result in physical death right away. Romans 6 is not telling us that when we sin, we will physically die. Rather, it is referring to spiritual death. Death, according to dictionary definitions, is a cessation of vital functions or a lack of life. Spiritual death is our natural state prior to accepting Christ as our savior. Ephesians 2:1-2 says, *[1]And you [He made alive when you] were [spiritually] dead and separated from Him because of your transgressions and sins, [2]in which you once walked. You were following the ways of this world [influenced by this present age], in accordance with the prince of the power of the air (Satan), the spirit who is now at work in the disobedient [the unbelieving, who fight against the purposes of God].*

> Jesus Christ is the permanent ruler of the whole world; Satan is only the temporary ruler of the part of the world that chooses to follow him.

The prince of the power of the air was understood, in this Scripture, by the Apostle Paul's readers to mean Satan. They believed that Satan and the evil spiritual forces inhabited the region between earth and sky. Satan is thus pictured as ruling an evil spiritual kingdom—the demons and those who are against Christ. Satan means the accuser. He is also called the devil. In the resurrection, Christ was victorious over Satan and his power. Therefore, Jesus Christ is the permanent ruler of the whole world; Satan is only the temporary ruler of the part of the world that chooses to follow him.

Colossians 2:13-14 says, *¹³When you were dead in your sins and in the uncircumcision of your flesh (worldliness, manner of life), God made you alive together with Christ, having [freely] forgiven us all our sins, ¹⁴having canceled out the certificate of debt consisting of legal demands [which were in force] against us and which were hostile to us. And this certificate He has set aside and completely removed by nailing it to the cross.*

Before we believed in Christ, our nature was evil. We disobeyed, rebelled, and ignored God (even at our best, we did not love Him with all our heart, mind, body, and soul). The Christian, however, has a new self. God has crucified the old rebellious nature (see Romans 6:6) and replaced it with a new loving nature. The penalty of sin died with Christ on the Cross. God has declared us not guilty, and we need no longer live under sin's power. God does not take us out of the world or make us robots—we will still feel like sinning, and sometimes we will sin. The difference is that before we were saved, we were slaves to our sinful nature, but now we are free to live for Christ (see Galatians 2:20).

The certificate of debt that was canceled was the legal demands of the Old Testament Law. The law opposed us by its demands for payment for our sin. Though no one can be saved by merely keeping that code, the moral truths and principles in the Old Testament still teach and guide today. We can enjoy our new life in Christ because we have joined Him in His death and resurrection. Our evil desires, our bondage to sin, and our love of sin died with Him. Now joining Him in His resurrected life, we may have unbroken fellowship with God and freedom from our sin. Our debt for sin has been paid in full; our sins are swept away and forgotten by God; and we can be clean and new. Spiritual death is a lack of spiritual life, an absence of proper spiritual functioning. God is the eternally existent One, the great *I AM* (see Exodus 3:14); He is life. Spiritual death is separation from God, who is life.

Second, when we are saved in Christ, we are rescued from ultimate spiritual death and brought into ultimate spiritual life. Romans 7:24 says, *Wretched and miserable man that I am! Who will [rescue me and] set me free from this body of death [this corrupt, mortal existence]?*

This inward struggle with sin was as real for Paul as it is for us. From Paul we learn what to do about it. Whenever Paul felt lost, he would return to the beginning of his spiritual life, remembering that he has already been freed by Jesus Christ. When you feel confused and overwhelmed by sin's appeal, follow Paul's example: Thank God that He has given you freedom through Jesus Christ. Let the reality of Christ's power lift you up to real victory over sin.

Third, even believers' sins will still result in a type of spiritual *death*. Though we are rescued from the ultimate penalty of sin (eternal separation from God), we are not exempt from the natural consequences of a broken relationship with the Father. When we sin, we experience the symptoms of spiritual death. We may feel guilty, empty, confused, or disconnected from God. We act as the unrighteous rather than as the righteous. Our sin, even as believers, hurts the heart of God and grieves His Spirit. I was a born-again believer and a leader in church who indulged in the sin of lust, *a whitewashed tomb full of dead man's bones.*

The condemnation *you are like whitewashed tombs* was part of Jesus' indictment of the scribes and Pharisees in Matthew 23. It is one of seven woes Jesus pronounced on the religious leaders as He confronted them about their hypocrisy. *Whitewashed tombs* mean exactly what it sounds like: tombs or mausoleums that have been covered with white paint, so they *look beautiful on the outside but on the inside are full of the bones of the dead and everything unclean* (see Matthew 23:27). This speaks to the spiritual condition of the scribes and Pharisees. Outwardly, they were holy and clean, but inside they were spiritually dead.

The comparison to whitewashed tombs would have been quite offensive because the Mosaic Law states, *Whoever touches the dead body of any person shall be unclean seven days* (see Numbers 19:11, ESV). For a group of people who prided themselves on ceremonial cleanliness and following the law, the accusation that they were full of dead bodies would be insufferable. That was precisely Jesus' point, though. They may have been ceremonially clean, but, inside, they were the highest level of unclean—full of the death and decay they tried so hard to avoid.

Such a harsh statement from Jesus reveals His anger at the hypocrisy in the religious leaders, who only cared about appearances. They took care of what people could see—and took pride in it—but they neglected what only God could see.

They *painted the outside*, leaving the inside full of greed and self-indulgence (see Matthew 23:25). In their eyes, if they followed the Law to the letter, they were holy, and the condition of their hearts wouldn't matter. Jesus needed to confront the superficiality of these dangerous leaders who did not practice what they preached. The whitewashed tombs were leading themselves and others to death and separation from God (see Matthew 23:15).

In the Sermon on the Mount, Jesus explained that the Law was less about what to do and not do and more about changing the heart. One analogy is that the law is like a mirror, revealing the flaws in man and how much they need God, like a mirror showing the food stuck between one's teeth. The law can reveal uncleanness, but it cannot be used to make a person righteous; only God can do that. The Pharisees were taking the mirror off the wall and trying to use it to pick their teeth. It simply does not work.

Whitewashed tombs work as a good contrast to Jesus Himself, the Son of Man, who came to bring life (see John 10:10). He offered rest and grace instead of the impossible burden and condemnation of the Pharisees (see Matthew 11:28–30). The superficial cleanness of whitewashed tombs cannot compare to the deep-cleansing blood of Christ (see 1 John 1:7). According to Ephesians 1:7, *In Him we have redemption [that is, our deliverance and salvation] through His blood, [which paid the penalty for our sin and resulted in] the forgiveness and complete pardon of our sin, in accordance with the riches of His grace.*

Ephesians 4:30 says, *And do not grieve the Holy Spirit of God [but seek to please Him], by whom you were sealed and marked [branded as God's own] for the day of redemption [the final deliverance from the consequences of sin].* The Holy Spirit within us is a seal or guarantee that we belong to God. The Holy Spirit is God's pledge guaranteeing that He will do what He has promised. The Holy Spirit is like a down payment, a deposit, a validating signature on the contract. The presence of the Holy Spirit in us demonstrates the genuineness of our faith, proves that we are God's children and secures eternal life for us. His power works in us to transform us now and what we experience now is a taste of the total change we will experience in eternity.

Though our sin, even as believers, does not sever our relationship with Him, our sin does put a barrier between us. Think of a child and a parent. When a child disobeys, the relationship with his parent is strained. The parent still loves the child and still has the child's best interest at heart. The child never stops belonging to the parent. However, the child may experience some consequences: mistrust, discipline, a sense of guilt, and the like. The relationship is ultimately restored, but generally pain comes first. So, it is with us and

God. When we rebel against God's rule in our lives, we rebel against life, and therefore experience *death* (a brokenness resulting in pain). When we return to God, we are also restored to spiritual life—communion with God, a sense of purpose, righteousness, freedom, and more. The rejoicing father in the Parable of the Prodigal Son said it best: *This son of mine was dead and is alive again* (see Luke 15:24).

I began to realize I had to recognize and stop making excuses about pornography and masturbation being a sin. They are both a form of fornication which is lust. I also had to agree with what God says about lust. I had to look to develop a desire for God over anyone or anything else. I was sick of my sin, and I wanted to take a self-assessment. I realized when we sin, it is the same as saying we love that sin more than we love God. That was a gut check and a hard pill to swallow. Did I love pornography and masturbation more than I loved God? So, I set out to overcome lust. BUT I failed! Did you catch the problem from the first sentence, I said: *I* set out to overcome lust. The problem in this sentence was the use of the word *I*. At this time, I was in my mid 20's and I knew; in the words of my mother, *I would surely bust hell wide open* if I didn't overcome the lustful desires that I struggled with.

> I failed miserably because I was trying to overcome a spiritual problem with natural methods.

As I stated before, I failed miserably because I was trying to overcome a spiritual problem with natural methods. Like sleeping with the light on or using willpower not to look at porn or masturbate but every time no matter how hard I tried or how guilty I felt about it afterward, I'd always end up viewing pornography and masturbating. The one thing I had to realize is what the root cause of these lustful desires were. We all experience lust in some way. Many times, we limit lust to the sexual realm but lust at its root is an unquenchable thirst for more and more. . . . money, fame, power, revenge, food, clothing, love. Unless our desires are turned over to the Lord, we will never be satisfied.

One day I remembered reading something about breaking strongholds and it was saying that you must break the silence and expose your secret sin. Satan uses our secrets to keep us in bondage and keep us in a cycle of sin. I had told one or two people that I struggled with lust, but I'd never gone into detail about it with anyone. One day I decided to break the silence and tell my therapist about my secret and how long it had gone on. Telling her gave me such freedom and that was the day that I knew I would be able to eventually overcome this spirit of lust.

Not only does Satan use our secrets to keep us in bondage and keep us in a cycle of sin, but he deceives us into believing our secret is really a secret. Guess what? Brace yourself, your secrets are not really secrets because God knows them all! Yes, God knows all your secrets!

Ezekiel 8:6-12 says, *⁶Furthermore, He said to me, "Son of man, do you see what they are doing, the great repulsive acts which the house of Israel is committing here, to drive Me far away from My sanctuary? But you will again see greater repulsive acts." ⁷Then He brought me to the entrance of the courtyard; and when I looked, behold, [there was] a hole in the wall. ⁸He said to me, "Son of man, now dig into the wall." And when I had dug into the wall, behold, there was an entrance. ⁹And He said to me, "Go in and see the wicked, repulsive acts that they are committing here." ¹⁰So I entered and looked and saw every kind of creeping things and beasts and loathsome things, and all the idols of the house of Israel, carved all around on the wall. ¹¹Standing before these [images] were seventy elders of the house of Israel, and among them stood Jaazaniah the son of Shaphan [the scribe], each man with his censer in his hand and a thick and fragrant cloud of incense was rising [as they prayed to these God's]. ¹²Then He said to me, "Son of man, do you see what the elders of the house of Israel do in the dark, each man in his [secret] room of carved images? For they say, 'The Lord does not see us; the Lord has abandoned the land.'"*

God showed Ezekiel all the things the people of Israel were doing in their secret places and in their dark rooms. God still saw them. Another important point to note in this scripture is where it says God was jealous. We know from Deuteronomy 6:15 that God is a jealous God, He wants it all. If we are giving our attention, desire, and focus to something other than Him then that means we are not being Spirit-led and we have turned away from Him to gratify our own fleshly desires. God is still the same as He was yesterday, and He saw me in my secret place, and He sees you in yours! In scene after scene, God revealed to Ezekiel the extent to which people had embraced idolatry and wickedness. God's Spirit works within us in a similar way, revealing sin that lurks in our lives. How comfortable would you feel if God held an open house in your life today?

I eventually overcame lust by crucifying my flesh and replacing the spirit of lust with the spirit of self-control. Galatians 2:20 says, *I have been crucified with Christ [that is, in Him I have shared His crucifixion]; it is no longer I who live, but Christ lives in me. The life I now live in the body I live by faith [by adhering to, relying on, and completely trusting] in the Son of God, who loved me and gave Himself up for me.* How have we been crucified with Christ? Legally, God looks at us as if we had died with Christ. Because our sins died with Him, we are no longer condemned (see Colossians 2:13-15). Relationally, we have become one with Christ, and His experiences are ours. Our Christian life began when, in unity with Him, we died to our old life.

Romans 6:5-11 says, *⁵For if we have become one with Him [permanently united] in the likeness of His death, we will also certainly be [one with Him and share fully] in the likeness of His resurrection. ⁶We know that our old self [our human nature without the Holy Spirit] was nailed to the cross with Him, in order that our body of sin might be done away with, so that we would no longer be slaves to sin. ⁷For the person who has died [with Christ] has been freed from [the power of] sin. ⁸Now if we have died with Christ, we believe that we will also live [together] with Him, ⁹because we know [the self-evident truth] that Christ, having been raised from the dead, will never die again; death no longer has power over Him. ¹⁰For the death that He died, He died to sin [ending its power and paying the sinner's debt] once and for all; and the life that He lives, He lives to [glorify] God [in unbroken fellowship with Him]. ¹¹Even so, consider yourselves to be dead to sin [and your relationship to it broken], but alive to God [in unbroken fellowship with Him] in Christ Jesus.*

The power and penalty of sin died with Christ on the Cross. Our old self, our sinful nature, died once and for all, so we are freed from its power. The body of sin is not the human body, but our rebellious sin-living nature inherited from Adam. Though our body willingly cooperates with our sinful nature, we must not regard the body as evil. It is the sin in us that is evil. And it is the power of sin at work in our body that is defeated. Paul has already stated that through faith in Christ we stand acquitted, not guilty before God. Here Paul emphasizes that we need no longer live under sin's power. As I stated before, God does not take us out of the world or make us robots—we still feel like sinning, and sometimes we will sin. The difference is we were slaves to our sinful nature before, but now we can choose to live for Christ.

Because of Christ's death and resurrection, His followers need never fear death, that assurance frees us to enjoy fellowship with Him and to do His will. This will affect all our activities—work, worship, play, Bible study, quiet times, and times of caring for others. When you know that you don't have to fear death, you will experience a new vigor in life.

Consider yourselves to be dead to sin means that we should regard our old sinful nature as dead and unresponsive to sin. Because of our union and identification with Christ, we are no longer obligated to carry out those old motives, desires, and goals. So let us consider ourselves to be what God has in fact made us. We have a new start, and the Holy Spirit will help us become in our daily experience what Christ has declared us to be. In our daily life, we must regularly crucify sinful desires that keep us from following Christ. This too, is a kind of dying with Him. And yet the focus of Christianity is not dying but living. Because we have been crucified with Christ, we have also been raised with Him. Legally, we have been reconciled with God and are free to grow into Christ's likeness. And in our daily life, we have Christ's resurrection power as we continue to fight sin. We are no longer alone, for Christ lives in us—He is our power for living and our hope for the future.

Remember the error I made when I first decided to try to deal with this spirit of lust. I tried to do it in my own strength, but we can never overcome sin in our own strength, we must rely fully and solely on the Son of God.

I sought God daily and began to study scriptures on lust, and in addition I figured out what my triggers were. My triggers were stress, feeling bad for myself, and watching or listening to anything sexual. I began to avoid things that would trigger a thought about sex. Notice, I said in addition! I would fall asleep with worship music playing because my bedroom was a trigger. I installed software on my computers, phone, and tablet and had people (and still have people) around me who have permission to ask me the hard questions and to whom I can remain accountable to in this area.

As I sought God, I realized I was using the wrong weapons to fight. Watching pornography led to masturbation. I am a highly visual person and I have a near photographic memory. I am also a highly auditory person and can remember things verbatim sometimes. I was trying to combat watching and hearing pornographic things by reading the Word and praying—which proved to be ineffective for me. God revealed

I needed to clean out the garbage the same way I was putting it in, so I started listening to the Bible on my phone, watching sermons, looking at animated depictions of Bible stores and listening to worship music. I started speaking the Word of God out loud and praying out loud. I started fighting differently and started seeing results almost immediately.

I also had to break ungodly soul ties that had been formed in my mind and in my spirit with porn stars through watching them over and over and fantasizing about them. Here is a short general prayer for breaking ungodly soul ties:

Father God in Heaven, thank You for revealing to me the presence of this/these soul tie(s) with (insert the name(s) of the person, place or thing below).

_____   _____

_____   _____

I confess, repent, and ask You to forgive me for my sin which activated this ungodly soul tie. I ask You to forgive me for any part I played in developing this ungodly soul tie.

By the power of the Holy Spirit and in the name of Jesus, I cancel this tie and cut it off from me. I command, in Jesus' name, that these persons/things have NO LEGAL ACCESS to my soul through ungodly means. My soul is set free from theirs and any sin, curses, or bondage that may have resulted from this tie. I command any spirits tied to this soul tie, to leave in Jesus' name. I bless those I just released from these soul ties and ask the Lord to bless them, for their salvation and forgive them for any part they have played in bringing the enemy's plan into my life.

I thank you, Father, that I am now free, in the strong Name of Jesus' I pray, Amen.

I don't want you to be discouraged, I want you to be encouraged and know that God has given you the ability to overcome anything in your life, including addictions like pornography and masturbation. I'm a living witness. Just know that to break the cycle of sin you must look for and press into God like never before. Be willing to let these things go and be willing to be open and transparent about your struggle, not only with God but with someone you know and trust who can hold you accountable. No matter how good it may feel, freedom in God and having a clean and pure heart will feel so much better! Also, think about how your testimony will be enhanced when you say you overcame lust!

I cannot stress enough for you to make sure you are in a good Bible-based church. Break the silence; realize your secret is not really a secret; get some accountability; and most importantly, seek, press into, and rely on God to help you overcome instead of trying to overcome in your own strength, because you will fail! When you're feeling discouraged or like you will never overcome lust, remember Romans 7:14-25 says, *¹⁴We know that the Law is spiritual, but I am a creature of the flesh [worldly, self-reliant—carnal and unspiritual], sold into slavery to sin [and serving under its control]. ¹⁵For I do not understand my own actions [I am baffled and bewildered by them]. I do not practice what I want to do, but I am doing the very thing I hate [and yielding to my human nature, my worldliness—my sinful capacity]. ¹⁶Now if I habitually do what I do not want to do, [that means] I agree with the Law, confessing that it is good (morally excellent). ¹⁷So now [if that is the case, then] it is no longer I who do it [the disobedient thing which I despise], but the sin [nature] which lives in me. ¹⁸For I know that nothing good lives in me, that is, in my flesh [my human nature, my worldliness—my sinful capacity]. For the willingness [to do good] is present in me, but the doing of good is not. ¹⁹For the good that I want to do, I do not do, but I practice the very evil that I do not want. ²⁰But if I am doing the very thing I do not want to do, I am no longer the one doing it [that is, it is not me that acts], but the sin[nature] which lives in me. ²¹So I find it to be the law [of my inner self], that evil is present in me, the one who wants to do good. ²²For I joyfully delight in the law of God in my inner self [with my new nature], ²³but I see a different law and rule of action in the members of my body [in its appetites and desires], waging war against the law of my mind and subduing me and making me a prisoner of the law of sin which is within my members. ²⁴Wretched and miserable man that I am! Who will [rescue me and] set me free from this body of death [this corrupt, mortal existence]?* ²⁵*Thanks be to God [for my deliverance] through Jesus Christ our Lord! So then, on the one hand I, myself with my mind serve the law of God, but on the other, with my flesh [my human nature, my worldliness, my sinful capacity—I serve] the law of sin.*

I know it sounds like a long tongue-twister but let's take a closer look. In verse 14 where Paul says, *but I am a creature of the flesh [worldly, self-reliant—carnal and unspiritual], sold into slavery to sin [and serving under its control]...* may be a reference to the old nature that seeks to rebel and be independent of God. If I, being a Christian, try to struggle with lust in my own strength, I am slipping into the grasp of sin's power.

> Becoming a Christian does not stamp out all sin and temptation from a person's life.

In verse 15, Paul shares three lessons that he learned in trying to deal with his own sinful desires. (1) Knowledge is not the answer. Paul felt fine if he did not understand what the Law demanded. When he learned the truth, he knew he was doomed. (2) Self-determination (struggling in one's own strength) doesn't work. Paul found himself sinning in ways that weren't even attractive to him. (3) Becoming a Christian does not stamp out all sin and temptation from a person's life. I was saved and a church leader during a large part of my struggle with masturbation and pornography.

This is more than the cry of one desperate man. It describes the experience of any Christian, like me, struggling against sin or trying to please God by keeping rules and laws without the Spirit's help. We must never underestimate the power of sin. We must never try to fight it in our own strength. Satan is a crafty tempter, and we have an amazing ability to make excuses. My excuse for watching pornography and masturbating stemmed from being raped and molested. I used the excuse of being afraid to have sex and justified my self-gratification. Instead of trying to overcome lust with human willpower, we must take hold of the tremendous power of Christ that is available to us. This is God's provision for victory over lust—He sends the Holy Spirit to live in us and give us power. And when we fall, He lovingly reaches out to help us up.

In verses 17-20, it appears Paul is saying, *the devil made me do it.* This sounds like a good excuse, but we are responsible for our actions. We must never use the power of sin or Satan as an excuse because they are defeated enemies. Without Christ's help, sin is stronger than we are, and sometimes we are unable to defend ourselves against its attacks. That is why we should never stand up to lust all alone. Jesus Christ, who has conquered sin once and for all, promises to fight by our side. If we look to Him for help, we will not have to give in to sin. Lastly, in verses 23-25, the *law in the members of my body* is the sin deep within us. This is our vulnerability to sin; it refers to the cycle of sin and everything within us that is more loyal to our old sinful way of selfish living than to God.

The inward struggle with the cycle of sin was as real for Paul as it is for us. From Paul, we learn what to do about it. Whenever Paul felt lost, he would return to the beginning of his spiritual life, remembering that he had already been freed by Jesus Christ. When you feel confused and overwhelmed by sin's appeal, follow Paul's example and thank God that He has given you freedom through Jesus Christ. Let the reality of Christ's power lift you up to real victory over the cycle.

Romans 7:14-25 talks about the sin struggle. That means you are not alone, God already knew what you would struggle with, and He has already provided you with a redeemer in Christ Jesus! Run to God! Repent, confess, kill your flesh daily and resist temptation! You can and will overcome lust because God has equipped you with what you need to break the cycle of sin.

Steps to Overcome Lust
1. Admit your weaknesses
2. Put on the Armor of God (see Ephesians 6:10–18)

Put on the Armor of God with this prayer based on Paul's exhortation in Ephesians 6:10–18:

Dear Heavenly Father, equip me:
- With the belt of truth. *May your truth rule in my heart, be in my mind and on my lips today.*
- With the breastplate of righteousness. *Apart from You there is no righteousness, but through Jesus I have been "born again" and made righteous in Your sight. May I live as a righteous person.*
- With feet fitted with the readiness that comes from the Gospel of peace. *May I reflect the Gospel in my words and actions, that through me, with my every encounter, others may be drawn one step closer to You.*
- With the shield of faith. *May I take You at Your Word concerning promises about the present and future— promises of everlasting love, abundant life, and so much more.*
- With the helmet of salvation. *Remind me that nothing can separate me from Your love and that I've been saved by grace. In Your grace, help me to say "no" to all ungodliness and worldly passions, and to live a self-controlled, upright, and godly life (see Titus 2:12,13).*
- And with the sword of the Spirit, the Word of God. *May Your Holy Spirit reign in my life and bring to my mind just the right Bible verses to be in my heart and on my lips.*

May I be "filled with the Spirit" and ready with Scripture as You were, Jesus, when the devil tempted You.
- *Finally, keep me in an attitude of prayer. Remind me to "pray in the Spirit on all occasions." Cause me to be alert and always pray for the saints; to be joyful and to give thanks in everything (see 1 Thessalonians 5:16-18).*

In Jesus' name I pray, Amen.

<small>Credit—Some content taken from *The Pray! Prayer Journal* by Dean Ridings</small>

3. Battle with Scripture
4. Set up Boundaries

A Prayer to Break Strongholds in Your Life

Heavenly Father, I come to You in the precious name of Jesus my Savior, whose shed blood is all-sufficient and able to free me from the powers and strongholds that have enslaved me. In the name of Jesus, I ask that You break the power of sin and lust in my life and the enslavement to all and any developed strongholds in me. Thwart the evil plans and purposes that the enemy has toward me—knowing that You are stronger and that Your plan for my life is perfect freedom, in Christ.

Lord, I am sorry that I have given Satan a foothold in my life and repent of the way I have allowed him to gain control. Break his power in me and fill me to overflowing with Your Holy Spirit. In my distress, I call on the name of the Lord Jesus and stand fast on the promises that NOTHING can separate me from the love of God, which is in Christ Jesus, my Lord. Break every stronghold in me and may I live to give You praise and glory from this day forward forevermore—in Jesus' name, Amen.

A Prayer to Overcome Lust
Dear Lord, I admit that I have sinned against you in my heart, mind, and actions. I have thought about and done things that do not please You. I feel guilty, dirty, and sinful. My God, I have been in this circle of pornography and masturbation for too long.

Lord Jesus, I ask Your forgiveness for my sins of masturbation and using pornography. I confess my sins and I turn away from them. I have tried quitting by myself, but it was to my own disappointment. I keep going back to watching pornography and masturbating, and the more I do it, the more I'm trapped in the act, and in guilt and shame.

I repent of my sin today, and I receive your forgiveness through Jesus Christ, my Savior. Purify my heart, mind, will, emotions, body, soul, and spirit. Create in me a clean heart, renew within me a steadfast spirit. Remove from me any ungodly thoughts. Restore your Holy Spirit to me. Let Your blood purify and renew my conscience. Set me free from guilt and shame. Give me a new identity in Christ, in the name of Jesus.

Lord, I invite You into my situation. You are my only hope. Come and do what only You can do. Set me free from watching pornography and masturbation. Every feeling of loneliness and lack of fulfillment making me watch pornography, let it break now, in the strong name of Jesus Christ.

Every spirit monitoring me and influencing me to watch pornography, be broken in the name of Jesus Christ. You evil spirit fighting my salvation, break now in the strong name of Jesus Christ. I'm redeemed and set free. I am the apple of God's eye and God's jealousy is on me. God, who does not sleep nor slumber, is watching over me. I am an obedient child of God, in the strong name of Jesus Christ. Amen!

Credit—https://christianstt.com/prayer-against-masturbation-and-pornography/

Declarations to Overcome Lust

I DECLARE there is an anointing of ease on my life. God is going before me making crooked places straight. His yoke is easy, and His burden is light. I will not continually struggle. What used to be difficult will not be difficult anymore. God's favor and blessing on my life are lightening the load and taking the pressure off. This is my declaration.

Chapter Four

Overcoming Impurity: Breaking Free from the Spirit of Conformity

*I*n our modern society, the concepts of *virginity* and being a *virgin* are often the subject of jokes and negative connotations. People often associated these concepts with being inexperienced, naive, unattractive, and/or not desirable. But what does the Bible have to say about this subject? The word *virgin* appears 33 times in the King James Version and 41 times in the New International Version. The Hebrew words thus translated are *bethuwlah* and *almah*. The Greek word is *parthenos*. When the Bible uses the word *virgin*, it refers to an unmarried person who has not had sexual relations.

Esther 2:2 says, *Then the king's attendants, who served him, said, "Let beautiful young virgins be sought for the king."*

Revelation 14:4 says, *These are the ones who have not been defiled [by relations] with women, for they are celibate. These are the ones who follow the Lamb wherever He goes. These have been purchased and redeemed from among men [of Israel] as the first fruits [sanctified and set apart for special service] for God and the Lamb.*

In today's culture, many people use the word virginity to express sexual purity; however, many others use a technical definition to find loopholes in moral standards. This limits the word to mean *the condition of never having gone all the way*—thus, a couple can do anything and everything short of sexual intercourse and still technically call themselves *virgins*. This is an unprofitable word game. Virginity (the state of never having had sexual intercourse), chastity (the state or practice of refraining from extramarital, or especially from all, sexual intercourse) and purity (freedom from immorality, especially of a sexual nature) should affect the heart, mind, and soul, not just certain body parts.

The Bible's emphasis is not so much on a technical or medical definition of virginity as it is on the condition of a person's heart. The morality we espouse (adopt or support a cause, belief, or way of life) and the actions we choose give evidence of our heart's condition. The Bible's standard is clear: abstinence before marriage and monogamy after marriage. I would like to take a moment to make a distinction between abstinence and celibacy.

Although many people use *celibacy* and *abstinence* interchangeably, there is a difference between the two terms. Abstinence usually refers to the decision not to have penetrative sex. It's typically limited to a specific period, such as until marriage. Celibacy is a vow to remain abstinent over an extended period. For some, this may mean their entire life.

There are three serious reasons to save sex for marriage. First, as believers, we are to obey what God tells us to do. First Corinthians 6:20 states, *You were bought with a price [you were actually purchased with the precious blood of Jesus and made His own]. So then, honor and glorify God with your body.* If we are in Christ, He has purchased us with the sacrifice of His life. He is our Lord, and we are to honor Him.

First Peter 1:15-16 says, *15But like the Holy One who called you, be holy yourselves in all your conduct [be set apart from the world by your godly character and moral courage]; 16because it is written, "You shall be holy (set apart), for I am holy."*

The God of Israel and of the Christian church is holy—He sets the standard for morality. Unlike the Roman God's, He is not warlike, adulterous, or spiteful. Unlike the God's of the pagan cults popular in the first century, He is not bloodthirsty or promiscuous. He is a God of mercy and justice who cares personally for each of His followers. Our holy God expects us to imitate Him by following His high moral standards. Like Him, we should be both merciful and just; like Him, we should sacrifice ourselves for others.

After people commit their lives to Christ, they usually still feel a pull back to their old ways. Peter tells us to be like our Heavenly Father—holy in all our behavior. Holiness mean being totally devoted or dedicated to God, set aside for His special use and set apart from sin and its influence. We're to be set apart and different, not blending in with the crowd, yet not being different just for the sake of being different. What makes us different are God's qualities in our lives. Our focus and priorities must be His. All this is in direct contrast to our old ways. We cannot become holy on our own, but God gives us His Holy Spirit to help us obey and to give us power to overcome sin. Don't use the excuse that you can't help slipping into sin. Call on God's power to free you from sin's grip.

Second, we are to fight our spiritual battles wearing the breastplate of righteousness. Ephesians 6:14 says, *So stand firm and hold your ground, having tightened the wide band of truth (personal integrity, moral courage) around your waist and having put on the breastplate of righteousness (an upright heart)...*

We are in a contest between our new nature in Christ and our fleshly desires. First Thessalonians 4:4 says *that each of you know how to control his own body in holiness and honor [being available for God's purpose and separated from things profane].* Allowing your body (rather than the Spirit) to control your actions is an act of defiance against God. Godly, loving sex between a husband and wife is giving and unselfish. Using someone to fulfill a desire of the flesh is self-centered and abusive. Even if the partner is willing, you are still helping him or her to sin and negatively altering that person's relationship with God and others.

The third and final reason involves the "mystery" of marriage. Ephesians 5:31-32 says, *[31]For this reason a man shall leave his father and his mother and shall be joined [and be faithfully devoted] to his wife, and the two shall become [a]one flesh. [32]This mystery [of two becoming one] is great; but I am speaking with reference to [the relationship of] Christ and the church.* The union of a husband and wife merges two people in such a way that little can affect one without also affecting the other. Oneness in marriage does not mean losing your personality in the other person. Instead, it means caring for your spouse as you care for yourself, learning to anticipate his or her needs, helping the other person become all he or she can be. The creation story tells of God's plan that husband and wife should be one (see Genesis 2:24), and Jesus also referred to this plan in Matthew 19:4-6.

When God spoke of two people being joined as one, He was referring to something we're only beginning to understand in a real, physiological way. When two people are intimate, the hypothalamus in the brain releases chemicals that induce feelings of attachment and trust. Having sex outside of marriage results in a person forming an attachment and trusting someone with whom he or she does not have a committed relationship. The definition of trust in the mind deteriorates. To have that kind of link with someone without the security of working together toward God is dangerous. Two individuals who are—even mildly—physiologically obsessed with each other but not committed to growing in God as a couple can be torn from God and His plans for them.

Conversely, if two people make a conscious, deliberate choice to commit to each other in marriage, and then allow the intimacy that releases these chemicals, the body can reaffirm the connection the mind has made. The physiological feelings of trust and attachment are reinforced by the reality of the relationship. In this way, two people become one physically, and that reflects what God has done spiritually.

Marriage is to model the relationship between the church and Christ. A married couple is to serve God in a strong, unified partnership. Sex, along with procreation, was designed by God to strengthen that partnership. Sex outside of marriage creates bonds that tear apart people's hearts instead of joining them together.

Finally, we need to remember a few things about virginity, and the lack thereof, given God's grace. Those who come to Christ after engaging in premarital sexual relationships are not virgins; however, they are fully cleansed by Christ now that they are saved. God can redeem anyone, and He can heal those who have indulged their fleshly lusts. For those who engaged in premarital sex after becoming a Christian, there is forgiveness in Christ. He can cleanse us from all unrighteousness and bring healing. In the horrible case of people victimized by sexual abuse or rape, who may feel that they, through no fault of their own, no longer measure up to the ideal standard of *virginity*, Christ is able to restore their spirit, heal their brokenness, and grant them wholeness.

First John 1:9 says, *If we [freely] admit that we have sinned and confess our sins, He is faithful and just [true to His own nature and promises] and will forgive our sins and cleanse us continually from all unrighteousness [our wrongdoing, everything not in conformity with His will and purpose].* Confession is supposed to free us to enjoy fellowship with Christ. It should ease our consciences and lighten our cares. But some Christians do not understand how this works. They feel so guilty that they confess the same sins over and over; then they wonder if they might have forgotten something. Other Christians believe that God forgives them when they confess, but if they died with unconfessed sins, they would be lost forever. These Christians do not understand that God *wants* to forgive us. He allowed His Beloved Son to die just so He could offer us pardon (the act of forgiving an offender, or removing the guilt of sin, that the punishment due to it may not be inflicted). When we come to Christ, He forgives all the sins we have committed and will ever commit. We don't need to confess the sins of the past all over again, and we don't need to fear that God will reject us if we don't keep our slate perfectly clean. Of course, we should continue to confess our sins, but not because failure to do so will make us lose our salvation. Our relationship with Christ is secure. Instead, we should confess so that we can enjoy maximum fellowship and joy with Him.

True confession also involves a commitment not to continue in sin. We wouldn't be genuinely confessing our sins to God if we planned to commit them again and just wanted temporary forgiveness. We should pray for strength to defeat temptation the next time we face it.

If God has forgiven us for our sins because of Christ's death, why must we confess our sins? In admitting our sins and receiving Christ's cleansing, we are: (1) agreeing with God that our sin truly is sin and that we are willing to turn from it, (2) ensuring that we don't conceal our sins from Him and consequently from ourselves, and (3) recognizing our tendency to sin and relying on His power to overcome it.

Chapter Four: Impurity

I explained this to tell you, *Hello, my name is LaKesha, and I am a virgin*. There was a time in my life when I would not have told people I was a virgin. There was even a time that I lied about being a virgin just to fit in and not feel awkward, immature, or viewed like I was inexperienced. Here is the thing though; being a virgin is not something that I should have been ashamed of for any reason. Let me pause and be clear, I am not condemning anyone who is not currently a virgin. This is my walk, and I am simply sharing my story.

For the former college students (and maybe some current ones) out there, remember going to the bookstore and purchasing books? Those books you purchased often came in shrink-wrapped packaging. The stipulation was that once you opened the package you could not return the book. This is an example of what *MY* virginity looks like. Admittedly I have some fingerprints on my packaging, however no one has opened the packaging yet. The only person who is permitted to open the package at this point is the one (my husband) who will pay the price for it, that price is called marriage!

I am not ashamed, or what I really should say is, I am no longer ashamed, I am grateful for all that I have been protected from by remaining a virgin. I am actually grateful for the ways of escape God has provided for me when I have placed myself in *hot & heavy* situations where the course of my life could have changed, and I would not be able to write this today.

Psalm 119:9 says, *How can a young man keep his way pure? By keeping watch [on himself] according to Your word [conforming his life to Your precepts].* We are drowning in a sea of impurity. Everywhere we look we find temptation to lead impure lives. The psalmist asked a question that troubles most of us: *How do we stay pure in a filthy environment?* We cannot do this on our own but must have counsel and strength more dynamic than the tempting influences around us. Where can we find that strength and wisdom? By reading God's Word and doing what it says.

I just want to encourage you today that your life is not about you. I have discovered that everything that has ever happened in my life only enhanced the testimony that I have been tasked to share to encourage others to overcome and win souls for Christ. You will experience so much freedom once you realize this.

Being a virgin, it's nothing to hide; I will scream it from the mountain tops only to give God the Glory. As unashamed as you are about sharing other things (on Social Media sites, or in conversation with friends and family), be that unashamed about sharing your faith and your testimony to help others overcome and ignite hope! Being a virgin is something that is sacred and special. I often compare being a virgin to seeing a unicorn.

A unicorn is believed to be this mythical creature that resembles a white horse with a horn on its head. In allegories, they are believed to be real but very rare and magical creatures. Unicorns supposedly represent harmony and purity and all things good. Did you know, the word unicorn is used in the Bible? A re'em, also reëm (Hebrew: רְאֵם), is an animal mentioned nine times in the Hebrew Bible. (see Job 39:9–10, Deuteronomy 33:17, Numbers 23:22, 24:8; Psalms 22:21, 29:6, 92:10; and Isaiah 34:7). It has been translated as unicorn in the King James Version, and in some Christian Bible translations as oryx wild ox, wild bull, buffalo or rhinoceros. Philosophers in Christian thought, say the unicorn represents the incarnation (the Christian belief that God took human form by becoming Jesus) of Christ, a symbol of purity and grace that could be captured only by a virgin.

Apparently, virgins nowadays are like unicorns. Again, I am 40 years old, and I am a virgin. I am not ashamed; I no longer feel like I am missing out on anything, and I am grateful that God has sustained and continues to sustain me to wait until marriage. However, when I am talking to people and sharing my story with them, I sometimes leave the conversation feeling like a unicorn. Some of the responses I get are hilarious and some are heartbreaking:

"Girl, I don't know how you do it!"
"Seriously?"
"So, you saying you have never ever had sex?"
"You should try it you might like it…"
"What are you waiting for?"

> No matter what culture says, purity honors God.

The list could go on and on, I believe at this point in my life I probably have heard every response there is ranging from encouraging to downright rude. Ultimately with believers and non-believers it is heartbreaking to see that something that should be regarded as sacred really isn't anymore. I want to speak directly to the women and men out there who feel like God has forgotten about you. The fact of the matter is God has not forgotten about you and He will honor your obedience in remaining a virgin and following His commands. No matter what culture says, purity honors God.

As I stated earlier, one of the questions I am asked is, *What are you waiting for?* This is probably the top one, so here are my top answers to this infamous question:

First, I want to honor God with my body. First Corinthians 6:19-20 tells us that our bodies are not our own so we can't give away what doesn't belong to us.

¹⁹Do you not know that your body is a temple of the Holy Spirit who is within you, whom you have [received as a gift] from God, and that you are not your own [property]? ²⁰You were bought with a price [you were actually purchased with the precious blood of Jesus and made His own]. So then, honor and glorify God with your body.

What did Paul mean when he said that our bodies belong to God? Many people say they have the right to do whatever they want with their own bodies. Although they think this is freedom, they are really enslaved to their own desires. When we become Christians, the Holy Spirit fills, and lives in us. Therefore, we no longer own our bodies. *Bought with a price* refers to slaves purchased at an auction. Christ's death freed us from sin, but also obligates us to His services. If you live in a building owned by someone else, you try not to violate the building's rules. Because your body belongs to God, you must not violate His standards for living.

The Scripture says *you were bought with a price*. When you go into a store and you see something you want, do you just take it? No, you don't, because taking something that you haven't paid for is called stealing! Instead, you do one of two things. You pay for it, or you work hard and save your money to pay for it later.

Having sex before marriage is stealing, and you are taking something that doesn't belong to you, and you haven't paid the price for. Our lives are not our own. Again, I call attention to another part in 1 Corinthians 6:19-20 where it says, *you are not your own*. We were created to worship God and to be loved by God and having sex before marriage is worshipping ourselves, gratifying our fleshly desires and exalting our flesh and the things of this world above a loving, merciful, and sovereign God.

Someone may be reading this thinking, *Wow! She is really going in!* Well, yes, I am because the Word of God is real, true, and it is the only thing I can rely on. So, why wouldn't I live by and apply all that God has commanded to me in His Word? So, to enhance my first reason I want to honor God with my body and keep His commands.

Second, I don't want to suffer the mental and emotional heartache, headache and drama that comes with having premarital sex. Sex is a beautiful thing, sex is great, and sex is wonderful. How do I know? I know because the Bible tells me so! However, outside of marriage sex can be complicated. The act of having sex is not just physical; the act of sexual intercourse is physical, mental, emotional, and spiritual, it's all-encompassing. That's why Genesis 2:24 (NLT) says, *For this reason a man shall leave his father and his mother and shall be joined to his wife; and they shall become one flesh.*

When the Bible says that two shall become one flesh, more is meant than what we would mean by the phrase, physical union. Genesis 2:24 gives us a picture of the marriage bond before sin entered the world. *One flesh* echoes the language of the preceding verse when Adam first meets Eve and exclaims, *This one is bone of my bone, and flesh from my flesh!* (see Genesis 2:23, NLT). Two becoming one in marriage involves uniting two whole and separate people into a new, God-designed, and God-purposed life.

The two shall become one flesh clause expresses the original purpose of marriage: to seal a permanent relationship between a husband and wife. Jesus spoke of this union in a conversation with the Pharisees about divorce: *"But at the beginning of creation God 'made them male and female. For this reason, a man will leave his father and mother and be united to his wife, and the two will become one flesh.' So, they are no longer two, but one flesh. Therefore, what God has joined together, let no one separate"* (see Mark 10:6–9; and Matthew 19:4–6).

Marriage was intended to be an unbreakable, lifelong union. Termination of marriage in divorce was not considered before sin came into the world (see Genesis 3). The Bible teaches that all instances of separation and divorce were because of sin (see Deuteronomy 24:1–4; Ezra 9—10; Malachi 2:14; Matthew 5:31–32; and Luke 16:18). When God said, *And the two shall become one*, His ideal objective was for the man and woman to join in an inseparable and exclusive union.

Husbands and wives become *one flesh;* not in the issuing and signing of the marriage license; not during the marriage ceremony but in sexual intimacy, as reflected literally in their children's lives. A child is one, new, whole, individual, and separate life created through the physical union of two people—a man and a woman. God's idyllic design for the sexual union in marriage is to be exclusive: "Give honor to marriage and remain faithful to one another in marriage. God will surely judge people who are immoral and those who commit adultery" (see Hebrews 13:4, NLT; Ephesians 5:22–33; 1 Timothy 3:2, 12 and Titus 1:6).

Two becoming one in the sexual aspect of marriage means caring for and fulfilling one another's physical needs with respect and mutual consent (see 1 Corinthians 7:1–5), not exploiting one another (see 1 Thessalonians 4:3–7) and delighting in one another (see Proverbs 5:15–19; and Ecclesiastes 9:9). God's design for physical intimacy in marriage is portrayed with beauty and dignity in the Song of Solomon.

Of course, oneness in marriage reaches far beyond the physical level. The original Hebrew word translated as "flesh" refers to much more than a person's physical or sexual composition. It relates to the whole of human existence. The biblical view of "one flesh" communicates a unity that covers every facet of a couple's joint lives as husband and wife. In marriage, two whole lives unite together as one emotionally, intellectually, financially, spiritually, and in every other way. The *two shall become one* in purpose. They are so close that they function like one person, balancing each other's strengths and weaknesses so that together they can fulfill their God-given calling.

In Scripture, marriage is viewed as a covenant relationship between a man and a woman (see Malachi 2:14–16; and Proverbs 2:16–17). The two people become dependent on each other and responsible for one another. This human bond in marriage is a metaphor for God's relationship with Israel (see Ezekiel 16:8) as well as a picture of the union between Christ and the church: *But whoever is united with the Lord is one with him in spirit* (see 1 Corinthians 6:17; and Ephesians 5:31–32).

Nevertheless, since the fall of humankind, the marriage relationship has failed to measure up to its God-intended ideal. Apart from salvation in Jesus Christ and the Holy Spirit's sanctifying work, husbands and wives cannot even begin to live in mutual harmony and accord. Yet, in Christ, believers discover the unconditional love of God (see 1 Corinthians 13:4–8)—a supernatural love that enables them to make a lifelong commitment to care for their spouse as Christ loved His bride, the church, and sacrificed Himself for her (see Ephesians 5:25).

The two shall become one flesh expresses the heart of the Bible's concept of marriage. By entering marriage, a husband and wife take solemn vows to become permanently one flesh—to love, honor, and cherish one another until they are parted by death.

First Corinthians 7:32-34 says, *[32]But I want you to be free from concern. One who is unmarried is concerned about the things of the Lord, how he may please the Lord; [33]but one who is married is concerned about the things of the world, how he may please his wife, [34]and his interests are divided. The woman who is unmarried, and the virgin, is concerned about the things of the Lord, that she may be holy both in body and spirit; but one who is married is concerned about the things of the world, how she may please her husband.*

Some single people feel tremendous pressure to be married. They think their lives can be complete only with a spouse. But Paul underlines one advantage of being single—the potential of greater focus on Christ and His work. If you are unmarried, use your special opportunity to serve Christ wholeheartedly.

I am about my Father's business and being Kingdom minded. I do not have time to unlawfully join to another as one flesh or be caught up in my feelings about a man who is not my husband. Premarital sex is a distraction and pulls us away from the will of God for our lives. It pulls us away from our purpose because we are too busy thinking about who we are sleeping with and what they are doing rather than being focused on the things of God and advancing the Kingdom of God.

Third, I don't want to have a child out of wedlock, and I don't want to contract any diseases or infections. I really don't think I need to elaborate much on this reason because it is self-explanatory.

If you haven't had sex yet, don't, eliminate and flee from temptation, ask God to sustain you and wait until marriage. If you have had sex, cry out to God with a repentant heart, confess, repent, and rededicate your body to God, eliminate and flee from temptation and ask Him to sustain you until marriage. We serve a loving, merciful, and forgiving God who sent his Son Jesus to die on the cross for all of us, and it is never too late for anyone to come back home to the arms of Jesus!

The Unicorn analogy was a lighthearted approach to a very serious issue. Virgins do exist, I know a couple and we believe in honoring God with our bodies, no we are not perfect, yes, we sometimes fall short, but God's grace and mercy is sufficient for us! Being a virgin isn't easy, but I know, one day, it will certainly be worth it!

I want to pray that these three things will be true for you. I didn't make these three things up. They come from a letter that Paul wrote to the Thessalonians. It was written to a city in Greece that was a bustling place. Because it was a trade city, it had many vices associated with trade. The theater there was known for being sexually crude. When you arrived, you would find that there was lots of alcohol, gambling, and sex. Those were a major part of the economy. Young men were expected to have an active sex life with slaves, prostitutes, and lovers. Bi-sexuality was more common in this area than in other parts of the empire. Friendships between men might be cemented with a sexual relationship. In other words, this was a sexual place. As Paul writes to them, he instructs them on how to be sexually pure in a sex-crazed culture. I see three things in this passage that form the basis of my prayer for you today.

First: I pray that you will become radically holy. First Thessalonians 4:1, says, ¹*Finally, believers, we ask and admonish you in the Lord Jesus, that you follow the instruction that you received from us about how you ought to walk and please God (just as you are actually doing) and that you excel* *even more and more [pursuing a life of purpose and living in a way that expresses gratitude to God for your salvation].*

Sexual standards were very low in the Roman empire, and in many societies today they are not any higher. The temptation to engage in sexual intercourse outside the marriage relationship has always been powerful. Giving in to that temptation can have disastrous results. Sexual sins always hurt someone: individuals, families, businesses, churches. Besides the physical consequences, there are also spiritual consequences.

Sexual desires and activities must be placed under Christ's control. God created sex for procreation and pleasure, and as an expression of love between a husband and wife. Sexual experience must be limited to the marriage relationship to avoid hurting ourselves, our relationship with God, and our relationships with others.

Second: I pray that you will be sexually pure. First Thessalonians 4:3-7 says, *³For this is the will of God, that you be sanctified [separated and set apart from sin]: that you abstain and back away from sexual immorality; ⁴that each of you know how to control his own body in holiness and honor [being available for God's purpose and separated from things profane], ⁵not [to be used] in lustful passion, like the Gentiles who do not know God and are ignorant of His will; ⁶and that [in this matter of sexual misconduct] no man shall transgress and defraud his brother because the Lord is the avenger in all these things, just as we have told you before and solemnly warned you. ⁷For God has not called us to impurity, but to holiness [to be dedicated, and set apart by behavior that pleases Him, whether in public or in private]."*

Sanctification, being made holy, is the process of living the Christian life. The Holy Spirit works in us, conforming us into the image of Christ (see Romans 8:29). So, according to 1 Thessalonians 4:3-7, here's what I pray for you: that as you live your life, and face temptation every single day, I want to pray that you will be sexually pure by:

- Abstaining from sexual immorality (4:3);
- Knowing how to control our bodies in holiness and honor (4:4);
- Avoiding stereotypical Gentile passions (4:5); and
- Not mistreating our "brothers and sisters" (4:6)

Third: I pray that you will base your holiness and purity on God. First Thessalonians 4:8 says, *So whoever rejects and disregards this is not [merely] rejecting man but the God who gives His Holy Spirit to you [to dwell in you and empower you to overcome temptation].* Sexual purity doesn't come naturally to anyone. Lean into the Holy Spirit's presence in your life. You are not alone. If you are a follower of Jesus Christ, you have not only been forgiven, but you have help.

God gave man and woman the joy and pleasure of sexual relations within the bounds of marriage, and the Bible is clear about the importance of maintaining sexual purity within the boundaries of that union between man and wife (see Ephesians 5:31). Humans are well aware of the pleasing effect of this gift from God but have expanded it well beyond marriage and into virtually any circumstance. The secular world's philosophy of "if it feels good, do it" pervades cultures, especially in the West, to the point where sexual purity is seen as archaic and unnecessary.

Yet look at what God says about sexual purity. *You should be sanctified: that you should avoid sexual immorality; that each of you should learn to control his own body in a way that is holy and honorable, not in passionate lust like the heathen, who do not know God. . . . For God did not call us to be impure, but to live a holy life* (see 1 Thessalonians 4:3–5, 7). This passage outlines God's reasons for calling for sexual purity in the lives of His children.

First, we are *sanctified*, and for that reason we are to avoid sexual immorality. The Greek word translated *sanctified* means literally *purified, made holy, consecrated [unto God]*. As Christians, we are to live a purified life because we have been made holy by the exchange of our sin for the righteousness of Christ on the cross and have been made completely new creations in Christ (see 2 Corinthians 5:17–21). Our old natures, with all their impurities, sexual and otherwise, have died, and now the life we live, we live by faith in the One who died for us (see Galatians 2:20). To continue in sexual impurity (fornication) is to deny that, and in doing so is, in fact, a legitimate reason to question whether we have ever truly been born again. Sanctification, the process by which we become more and more Christlike, is essential evidence of the reality of our salvation.

We also see in 1 Thessalonians 4:3–5 the necessity of controlling our bodies. When we give in to sexual immorality, we give evidence that the Holy Spirit is not filling us because we do not possess one of the fruits of the Spirit—self-control. All believers display the fruit of the Spirit (see Galatians 5:22–23) to a greater or lesser degree depending on whether or not we are allowing the Spirit to have control. Uncontrolled *passionate lust* is a work of the flesh (see Galatians 5:19), not of the Spirit. So, controlling our lusts and living sexually pure lives is essential to anyone who professes to know Christ. In doing so, we honor God with our bodies (see 1 Corinthians 6:18–20).

We know God's rules and discipline reflect His love for us. Following what He says can only help us during our time on earth. By maintaining sexual purity before marriage, we avoid emotional entanglements that may negatively affect future relationships and marriages. Further, by keeping the marriage bed pure (see Hebrews 13:4), we can experience unreserved love for our mates, which is surpassed only by God's enormous love for us.

The gospel is not the story of Christ loving a pure bride who loves him; it's the story of Christ's love for a whore who thinks she has nothing to offer and keeps giving herself to others. —Ray Ortlund

God wants you to glorify Him by living in purity. This story of Joseph is a great example of how to actively guard your heart from impurity. Genesis 39:7-12 says, *7Then after a time his master's wife looked at Joseph with desire, and she said, "Lie with me." 8But he refused and said to his master's wife, "Look, with me in the house, my master does not concern himself with anything; he has put everything that he owns in my charge. 9He is not greater in this house than I am, nor has he kept anything from me except you, because you are his wife. How then could I do this great evil and sin against God [and your husband]?" 10And so it was that she spoke to Joseph [persistently] day after day, but he did not listen to her [plea] to lie beside her or be with her. 11Then it happened one day that Joseph went into the house to attend to his duties, and none of the men of the household was there in the house. 12She caught Joseph by his [outer] robe, saying, "Lie with me!" But he left his robe in her hand and ran and got outside [the house].*

Potiphar's wife failed to seduce Joseph, who resisted this temptation by saying it would be a sin against God. Joseph didn't say, *I'd be hurting you,* or *I'd be sinning against Potiphar,* or *I'd be sinning against myself.* Under pressure, such excuses are easily rationalized away. Remember that sexual sin is not just between two consenting adults. It is an act of disobedience against God.

Joseph avoided Potiphar's wife as much as possible. He refused her advances and finally fled from her. Sometimes merely trying to avoid temptation is not enough. We must turn and run, especially when the temptations seem very strong, as is often the case in sexual temptation.

Overcoming impurity and the urge to conform to the world's standards took some time for me, but it was my desire to develop true intimacy with God that helped me break free from the spirit of conformity.

My virginity and purity are something to be regarded as priceless and sacred not bargain bin and worthless. And not just something I am saving for my husband because it's so much deeper than that. I am waiting until marriage for sex, and I endeavor to live a pure lifestyle because my choices now are impacting generations to come.

Recently, God has been speaking to me about purity even the more through open visions and dreams. You can be an impure virgin, as I was. Remember purity is a heart posture. One thing He revealed to me is that He has sustained me and taken me through a purification process because from my husband and I will emerge a pure, brand-new bloodline. One morning after and open vision, God downloaded these words to me:

Your husband is going to be tall and handsome beyond your wildest dreams. He is going to love you, adore you and literally treat you like a queen. You will literally and figuratively experience things with him you've never experienced before and do things you've never done before. You will feel so, so, so, so, loved, safe, secure and taken care of. You will be so in love with him. You will like him, respect him, laugh with him, and honor him. He is going to be so fine. Your life will be like a dream every day. Why, because you waited. Because you waited, your marriage, and your husband will be your reward. You will continue to do ministry and he will support you. You will do ministry together and impact and influence many through a purity ministry, not like the popular purity culture that sprang up years ago but a ministry about how to live pure and purify your bloodline. A ministry about how to be a kingdom man and a kingdom woman who comes together to create a kingdom family with a pure bloodline free of generational curses and habitual sin.

Because of my choice, my bloodline will reap the benefits.

Steps to Overcome Impurity

1. Place God's feelings above your own feelings. Joseph strongly cared about not sinning against God. He thought about God's feelings first and what God would think about his action.

2. Stop trying to make exceptions. For example, in a dating relationship instead of asking how far is too far, ask how can my relationship honor God? Joseph did not see how far he could take this relationship with his master's wife. He made no excuses, no exceptions.

3. Avoid tempting situations. Joseph tried never to put himself into situations that would tempt him. He knew where and what would tempt him so he would flee the scene. If you do happen to get into a bad situation, remember that God never leaves you there with no ways to escape. Listen to the Holy Spirit.

4. Set boundaries. Always know your boundaries before you get into a situation. I heard a pastor say once, *Once you're in the back seat of that car, it will be easier to push your*

boundaries. Make sure to set them in advance. Have you experienced this for yourself? You don't have to be in a car, but you know what I mean—it is harder to stop once you start.

If it's a person who tempts you, then don't spend alone time with them. If it's sexual scenes in movies or TV shows, then don't watch them. If it's your computer or phone, then only use it in a public room of your house. Set boundaries for yourself to help guard your heart from impurity.

5. Take radical steps to pursue purity. In the story, Joseph left his robe and ran, probably clothed only in underwear (or nothing at all)! That is how important it was for him to—literally—flee from temptation. As a result, he was thrown into jail.

A Prayer to Overcome Impurity
Dear Lord, help me be holy and stay away from sexual sin so that I won't be a slave to my passions. Help me live in the holiness that honors You. Help me not to fall into the traps of being a human with a sinful nature. Help me not to make myself impure by dabbling in idolatry, sorcery, hostility, quarreling, jealousy, uncontrolled anger, greed, selfish ambition, dissension, division, envy, or drunkenness. For these things bring pain to me and others. I desire to live with You, Lord, as my focus as I help the neighbors all around me as much as I can. Purity will show in my life when I live with patience, kindness, and sincere love. Then I

can testify to the power of the Holy Spirit that enables me to do any good deed. Help me be an example to others in what I say and how I live and love. Help me not to focus only on my own interests, but to take much interest in others. May I always strive to walk in this purity.

Help me remember that what I focus on will always affect me. May I focus on You more than I look at the worthless things in this world. Give me discernment to know what is worthy to look at and what is not. My eyes are like lamps. They can let light into my heart and soul. May I take in as much of Your light and truth as possible, while looking away from dark things. The world is such a fallen place that sometimes I cannot stop myself from seeing things that corrupt me. But I can stop it at the point of seeing before it becomes a lingering issue.

Finally, Lord, help me run from the evil things in this world. Help me run from some of the innocuous things that may not be evil but consume too much of my precious time. My thoughts can become actions, so help me have pure thoughts. Help my thoughts to be of You and Your Word most of the time, so I can live a pure and godly life of faith and perseverance. I want to fix my thoughts on things that are pure, true, honorable, right, and lovely as much as possible. For those thoughts encourage me to go forward in faith and hope. The more I think about good things, the more I will do good deeds. In the strong name of Jesus I pray, Amen.

Credit: https://www.crosswalk.com/faith/prayer/a-prayer-for-purity-in-every-part-of-our-lives.html

Declarations to Overcome Impurity

I WILL seek first God's kingdom and righteousness in every aspect of my life.

I WILL seek to love God with all my heart, all my soul, all my mind, and all my strength.

I WILL seek to daily study, meditate, and memorize God's Word.

I WILL seek to daily prepare my mind for battle, taking captive every thought to make them fully obedient to Christ, and thinking only on those things that glorify God.

I WILL seek to control my own body in a way that is holy and honorable, abstaining from the sinful desires of my flesh and avoiding all forms of sexual immorality or any kind of impurity.

I WILL NOT look lustfully at a man or woman.

I WILL NOT allow my TV, computer or handheld devices, movies, books, magazines, or any other form of entertainment to set before my eyes any ungodly image or standard.

I WILL regularly seek the support of godly men/women who will hold me accountable to this commitment.

I WILL fight the good fight, I WILL finish the race, I WILL keep the faith!

Chapter Five

Overcoming Sickness: Breaking Free from the Spirit of Unrest

Be still before the Lord; wait patiently for Him and entrust yourself to Him; Do not fret (whine, agonize) because of him who prospers in his way, Because of the man who carries out wicked schemes.
Psalm 37:7

Matthew 11:28-30 says, *28Come to Me, all who are weary and heavily burdened [by religious rituals that provide no peace], and I will give you rest [refreshing your souls with salvation]. 29Take My yoke upon you and learn from Me [following Me as My disciple], for I am gentle and humble in heart, and you will find rest (renewal, blessed quiet) for your souls. 30For My yoke is easy [to bear] and My burden is light.* A yoke is a heavy wooden harness that fits over the shoulders of oxen. It is attached to a piece of equipment that oxen pull. A person may be carrying heavy burdens of (1) sin, (2) excessive demands, (3) oppression and persecution, or (4) weariness.

Jesus frees people from all these burdens. The rest that Jesus promises is love, healing, and peace with God, not the end of all labor or suffering. A relationship with God changes meaningless, wearisome toil into spiritual productivity and purpose. Let me tell you how God did that for me.

In June of 2017, I began having pelvic discomfort. I felt as if my entire pelvic area was burning constantly, and I had shooting pain on the right side. All I could think was, *Okay God, I have one ovary and one uterus that I'll need to have a child, so what's the deal?* Yes, I was jumping to conclusions before I knew anything at all.

Years prior I had several ovarian cysts that lead to the removal of my left ovary. I was so heartbroken during that time because I've always wanted to have children, but God spoke to me back then and said I would have children.

Fast forward, the burning and pain only felt like it was getting worse so, reluctantly I scheduled an appointment with my gynecologist. The doctor recommended I have a transvaginal sonogram done. By this time, I had no rest or peace in my spirit. Satan was having a field day in my mind. Although I was afraid of what the results would be, I got the sonogram.

Let's stop for a moment and talk about the spirit of fear. Often when we are faced with sickness, the number one emotion we experience is fear. Merriam-Webster defines fear as an unpleasant often strong emotion caused by anticipation or awareness of danger. We listen to people; we listen to the doctors' reports, and we begin to form opinions and believe things that may not be true in the supernatural. It's almost as if we stop believing God's' Word and we believe the doctors' word instead. Fear comes, and we tend to run with that fear and let it control us and form beliefs that we will never be healed. We must have an attitude like Job in chapter 13, verse 15 where he said, *¹⁵Even though He kills me; I will hope in Him. Nevertheless, I will argue my ways to His face.* With all that happened to Job, he did not let fear overtake him. Instead, he rested in Christ, stood on God's Word, and trusted Him to bring him through.

One Friday about two weeks after the sonogram was done, I received a call from my gynecologist and he informed me that the lining of my uterus was thicker than normal, and I had an ovarian cyst on the right side which would require surgery.

My heart sank. For 12 years things were fine, and I'd experienced no gynecological issues, I was perplexed, to say the least. God tests and tries; Satan tempts and taunts. All those years ago God said I would have children and I believed Him. My thoughts were full of questions, I was even angry with God. Here I was walking in His purpose for my life, serving and pursuing Him and He has the nerve to let this illness befall me. I was pissed!

Isn't it funny how when things are going well, we don't have a problem trusting God fully and resting in Him? Yet, as soon as trouble comes, we have the audacity to be upset with God for throwing what we perceive as a monkey wrench into our lives. Who said once we gave our lives to Christ every day would be a cakewalk? Who said that we wouldn't suffer or endure tests and trials? I don't remember reading that anywhere in the Bible, in fact, the Word of God says the exact opposite.

James 1:2-8 says, *²Consider it nothing but joy, my brothers and sisters, whenever you fall into various trials. ³Be assured that the testing of your faith [through experience] produces endurance [leading to spiritual maturity, and inner peace]. ⁴And let endurance have its perfect result and do a thorough work, so that you may be perfect and completely developed [in your faith], lacking in nothing. ⁵If any of you lacks wisdom [to guide him through a decision or circumstance], he is to ask of [our benevolent] God, who gives to everyone generously and without rebuke or blame, and it will be given to him. ⁶But he must ask [for wisdom] in faith, without doubting [God's willingness to help], for the one who doubts is like a billowing surge of the sea that is blown about and tossed by the wind. ⁷For such a person ought not to think or expect that he will receive anything [at all] from the Lord, ⁸being a double-minded man, unstable and restless in all his ways [in everything he thinks, feels, or decides].*

In verses 2-3, James doesn't say if you face trials, but when you face them. He assumes that we will have trials and that it is possible to profit from them. The point is not to pretend to be happy when we face pain or sickness, but to have a positive outlook (*consider it all joy*) because of what trials can produce in our lives. James tells us to turn our hardships into times of learning. Tough times can teach us perseverance.

So, this sickness that God was allowing wasn't a punishment or consequence of anything I'd done or not done; it was a way to get my attention and to show me myself so that I may see more of Him. We can't really know the depth of our character until we see how we react under pressure. It is easy to be kind to others when everything is going well, but can we still be kind when others are treating us unfairly? Will we still love God when we feel He is placing more on us than we can bear? God wants to make us mature and complete, not keep us from all pain. Instead of complaining about our struggles, we should see them as opportunities for growth. Thank God for promising to be with you through rough times. Ask Him to help you solve your problems or to give you the strength to endure them. Then be patient. God will not leave you alone with your problems; He will stay close and help you grow.

In verse 5, James talks about wisdom. By wisdom, James is talking about not only knowledge but about the ability to make wise decisions in difficult circumstances. Where we need wisdom, we can pray to God, and He will supply what we need. Whether it is wisdom, peace, rest, or provision, He will generously supply. Christians don't have to grope around in the dark, hoping to stumble upon answers. We can ask for God's' wisdom to guide our choices.

Wisdom means practical discernment. It begins with respect for God, leads to right living, and results in increased ability to tell right from wrong. God is willing to give us this wisdom, but we will be unable to receive it if our goals are self-centered instead of God-centered. To learn God's' will, we need to read His Word and ask Him to show us how to obey it. Then we must do what He tells us to do.

In verse 6, to *ask in faith without any doubting* means not only to believe in the existence of God but also to believe in His loving care. It includes relying on God and expecting that He will hear and answer when we pray. We must put away our critical attitude when we come to Him. God does not grant every thoughtless or selfish request. We must have confidence that God will align our desires with His purposes. My desire was to have children, but I had to ask myself, how does that align with God's purposes for my life and if He didn't grant my desire to have children would I be okay with that?

The ability to have children or not was the real issue for me. God said I would but if He didn't allow it the way I wanted, when I wanted would that change my love for Him, would that change the way I serve, the way I teach or how my walk with Him looks? This is what God was showing me about myself. Were my devotion and love conditional? All these thoughts and emotions were enveloping me, my heart and mind were a mess. I was being shillyshally (irresolute, undecided, or hesitating manner) about what I knew of God and His ways, which caused a great amount of unrest leading up to the surgery.

A mind that wavers is not completely convinced that God's way is best. It treats God's Word like any human advice, and it retains the choice to disobey. It vacillates between allegiance to subjective feelings, the worlds ideas, doctor's reports, and God's commands. If your faith is new, weak, or struggling, remember that you can trust and rest in God. Then be loyal to Him. To stabilize your wavering or doubtful mind, commit yourself wholeheartedly to God.

God was requiring that I rest in Him, constantly and consistently. My trust, peace and rest were conditional upon whether I was experiencing hardship or not. When things were good, there was rest, and I could trust God completely, but when things were not good, I would doubt and waver in my belief in Him. He allowed this test, this sickness, and hardship to reveal the error of my ways.

If you have ever seen the constant rolling of huge waves at sea, you know how restless they are—subject to the forces of wind, gravity, and tide. Doubt leaves a person as unsettled as the waves. If you want to stop being tossed about, rely on God to show you what is best for you. Ask Him for wisdom, and trust that He will give it to you. Then your decisions will be sure and solid.

The surgery was scheduled for September 22, 2017, at 10:00 am. Surprisingly I was not afraid, and I was at peace. The days leading up to the surgery God had performed a spiritual surgery to remove the tumor of doubt and double mindedness. He allowed me to rest knowing that whatever the outcome of this surgery, He was in control, and I could rest completely in Him.

So how do we break the spirit of unrest, Hebrews 4:1-5 tells us, *¹Therefore, while the promise of entering His rest still remains and is freely offered today, let us fear, in case any one of you may seem to come short of reaching it or think he has come too late. ²For indeed we have had the Good News [of salvation] preached to us, just as the Israelites also [when the Good News of the promised land came to them]; but the message they heard did not benefit them, because it was not united with faith [in God] by those who heard. ³For we who believe [that is, we who personally trust and confidently rely on God] enter that rest [so we have His inner peace now because we are confident in our salvation, and assured of His power], just as He has said, "As I swore [an oath] in My wrath, They shall not enter My rest," [this He said] although His works were completed from the foundation of the world [waiting for all who would believe]. ⁴For somewhere [in Scripture] He has said this about the seventh day: "And God rested on the seventh day from all His works"; ⁵and again in this, "They shall not enter My rest."* We can paraphrase this verse in this way: God makes it possible for us to enter His rest, so we need to make sure that we accept His offer. If we do not keep our faith in Him, we will fail to enter.

Some of the Jewish Christian who received this letter may have been on the verge of turning back from their promised rest in Christ, just as the people in Moses' day had turned back from the promised land. In both cases, the difficulties of the present moment overshadowed the reality of God's promise, and the people doubted that God would fulfill His promises. When we trust our own efforts instead of Christ's power, we too are in danger of turning back. Our own efforts are never adequate, only Christ can see us through.

The Israelites of Moses' day illustrate a problem facing many who fill our churches today. They know a great deal about Christ, but they do not know Him personally—they don't combine their knowledge with faith. Let the Good News about Christ help your life. Believe in Him and then act on what you know. Trust in Christ and do what He says.

God rested on the seventh day, not because He was tired, but to show the completion of creation. The world was perfect, and God was well satisfied with it. This rest is a foretaste of our eternal joy when creation will be renewed and restored, every mark of sin will be removed, and the world will be made perfect again. Our Sabbath rest in Christ begins when we trust Him to complete His good and perfect work in us.

Hebrews 11:1 says, *¹Now faith is the assurance (title deed, confirmation) of things hoped for (divinely guaranteed), and the evidence of things not seen [the conviction of their reality—faith comprehends as fact what cannot be experienced by the physical senses].* Do you remember how you felt when you were young, and your birthday approached? You were excited and anxious. You knew you would certainly receive gifts and other special treats. But some things would be a surprise. Birthdays combine assurance and anticipation, and so does faith! Faith is the conviction based on past experiences that God's' new and fresh surprises will surely be ours.

In addition to assurance, another word that describes faith is conviction. These qualities need a secure beginning and ending point. The beginning of faith is believing in God's

Character. Remember when I said, the sickness came to get my attention and to show me myself so that I may see more of Him: Seeing more of Him meant recognizing and believing in His Character—He is who He says. The end of faith is believing in God's promises—He will do what He says. When we believe that God will fulfill His promises even though we don't see those promises materializing yet, we demonstrate true faith.

So, how do we enter this rest talked about in Hebrews? Verse 2 tells us, *²For indeed we have had the Good News [of salvation] preached to us, just as the Israelites also [when the Good News of the promised land came to them]; but the message they heard did not benefit them, because it was not united with faith [in God] by those who heard.* The author urges us to be diligent, then he talks about *the Good News*. This implies that we enter God's rest by means of the Gospel—The Word of God.

The Word of God is the key to breaking the spirit of unrest and entering the sweet rest that can only come from our Lord and Savior Jesus Christ. The Word of God is our GPS, our instruction manual and it is our guide not only for how to live this life but to live this life resting in God.

Here are a few scriptures from our GPS that give us direction:

Matthew 16:24 tells us, *²⁴Then Jesus said to His disciples, "If anyone wishes to follow Me [as My disciple], he must deny himself [set aside selfish interests], and take up his cross [expressing a willingness to endure whatever may come] and follow Me [believing in Me, conforming to My example in living and, if need be, suffering or perhaps dying because of faith in Me].* When Jesus used this picture of his followers taking up their crosses to follow Him, the disciples knew what He meant. Crucifixion was a common Roman method of execution, and condemned criminals had to carry their crosses through the streets to the execution site. Following Jesus, therefore, meant a true commitment, the risk of death, and no turning back.

Isaiah 30:21 says, *Your ears will hear a word behind you, "This is the way, walk in it," whenever you turn to the right or to the left.* When the people of Jerusalem left God's path, He would correct them. He will do the same for us. But when we hear His voice of correction, we must be willing to follow it!

> But God knows what is best for us. He is a better judge of what we want than we are!

Proverbs 3:5-6 (NASB) tells us, *5Trust in the Lord with all your heart and do not lean on your own understanding. 6In all your ways acknowledge Him, And He will make your paths straight.* Leaning has the sense of putting your whole weight on something, resting on and trusting in that person or thing. When we have an important decision to make, we sometimes feel that we can't trust anyone—not even God. But God knows what is best for us. He is a better judge of what we want than we are! We must trust Him completely in every choice we make. We should not omit careful thinking or belittle our God-given ability to reason, but neither should we trust our own ideas to the exclusions of all others. We must not be wise in our own eyes. We should always be willing to listen to and be corrected by God's Word and wise counselors. Bring your decisions to God in prayer, use the Bible as your guide, and then follow God's leading. He will make your paths straight by both guiding and protecting you.

To receive God's guidance, said Solomon, we must acknowledge God in all our ways. This means turning every area of life over to Him. About a thousand years later, Jesus emphasized the same truth in Matthew 6:33. Look at your values and priorities. What is important to you? In what areas have you not acknowledged Him? What is His advice? In many areas of your life, you may already acknowledge God, but it is the areas where you attempt to restrict or ignore His influence that will cause you grief. Make Him a vital part of everything you do; then He will guide you because you will be working to accomplish His purposes.

In Psalm 37:23-24, *²³The steps of a [good and righteous] man are directed and established by the Lord, And He delights in his way [and blesses his path]. ²⁴When he falls, he will not be hurled down, Because the Lord is the One who holds his hand and sustains him.* The person in whom God delights is one who follows God, trusts Him, and tries to do His will. God watches over and makes firm every step that person takes. If you would like to have God direct your way, then seek His advice before you step out.

In Proverbs 16:9, *⁹A man's mind plans his way [as he journeys through life], But the Lord directs his steps and establishes them.*

And Isaiah 43:19 says, *¹⁹"Listen carefully, I am about to do a new thing, now it will spring forth; Will you not be aware of it? I will even put a road in the wilderness, Rivers in the desert."*

Isaiah 48:17 reminds us, *¹⁷This is what the Lord, your Redeemer, the Holy One of Israel says, "I am the Lord your God, who teaches you to profit (benefit), Who leads you in the way that you should go."* Like a loving parent, God teaches and directs us. We should listen to Him because peace and righteousness come to us as we obey His Word. Refusing to pay attention to God's commands invites punishment and threatens that peace and righteousness.

Across these Scriptures you see a couple common themes begin to emerge of trust, faith, and sacrifice. To find rest, we must trust God to guide us, have faith that He has our best interest in mind and sometimes we have to sacrifice the things we want for the things He wants. Remember, God had spoken to me and said I would have children, so why was I tripping? This reminds me of the story of Abraham and Isaac. I lacked trust, faith and I was not willing to sacrifice what I wanted and had been waiting for.

Genesis 12 begins the story of Abraham (then called Abram) and his barren wife Sarah (then called Sarai). Verses 1 through 4 record God's first words to him about a homeland for his offspring. Even though the gift of a son is not directly mentioned in this first communication, God hinted at His plan for Abram. Abraham was 75 years old when he first received the promise, and Genesis 21:5 tells us he was 100 years old when Isaac was born. Sarah was 90. So, Abraham and Sarah waited 25 years for the fulfillment of God's promise.

In those 25 years between the time that Abram was promised a son and the birth of Isaac, Abram and Sarah had certain ideas of how they might facilitate the keeping of the promise. One was that Abraham's steward, Eliezer, would become the heir of Abraham's household (see Genesis 15:2–3). Another idea was that Abraham could have an heir through a son conceived by Sarah's slave, Hagar (see Genesis 16:1–2). In both cases, God rejected those men as Abraham's heirs, pointing Abraham and Sarah to a literal, miraculous fulfillment of the promise.

Abraham is called the father of faith (see Romans 4:11–12) because of his response to God both in leaving his homeland and receiving a son in his old age. Genesis 15:4–5 again describes God's promise to Abraham that his offspring would be as *the sands of the sea*. Even though Abraham was old and had no sons, he never doubted that God would do as He promised. He did not understand how such a thing could be possible, but he humbly accepted God's word as truth.

Genesis 15:6 lays out the truth that salvation is by faith, apart from works: *Abram believed the Lord, and he credited it to him as righteousness.* Romans 4:3–5 and Galatians 3:5–7 elaborate on this truth. Just as Abraham was counted as righteous before he did anything worthy of praise, so we are counted as righteous by simply believing that the sacrifice of Jesus Christ is sufficient payment for our sin (see 2 Corinthians 5:21).

However, that faith produces actions that validate it. James 2:14–18 helps us understand the kind of faith Abraham had. It was a faith that acted. He moved because God said to move. He trusted because God said to trust. He prepared to welcome a son because God promised him a son. By acting on his faith, Abraham proved that he trusted God, and that trust was credited to his account. His faith in the promises of God saw him through years of waiting. He never doubted God's goodness or His word, and, for that, God considered him righteous.

Abraham had obeyed God many times in his walk with Him, but no test could have been more severe than the one in Genesis 22. God commanded, "Take your son, your only son, whom you love—Isaac—and go to the region of Moriah. Sacrifice him there as a burnt offering on a mountain I will show you" (see Genesis 22:2).

This was an astounding command because Isaac was the son of promise. God had promised several times that from Abraham's own body would come a nation as multitudinous (very numerous) as the stars in Heaven (see Genesis 12:2–3; and 15:4–5). Later, Abraham was specifically told that the promise would be through Isaac (see Genesis 21:12).

Given that God's testing of Abraham involved a command to do something He elsewhere forbids (see Jeremiah 7:31), we must ask, *Why did God command Abraham to sacrifice Isaac?* The Bible does not specifically address the answer to this question, but in our study of Scripture we can compile a few reasons:

God's command to sacrifice Isaac was to test Abraham's faith. God's tests prove and purify our faith. They cause us to seek Him and trust Him more. God's test of Abraham allowed His child—and all the world—to see the reality of faith in action. Faith is more than an inner spiritual attitude; faith works (see James 2:18).

God's command to sacrifice Isaac was to validate Abraham as the *father* of all who have faith in God. *Abraham's faith was credited to him as righteousness* (see Romans 4:9). And we today *who have the faith of Abraham* also find that *he is the father of us all* (verse 16). Without Abraham's response to the command to sacrifice Isaac, we would have difficulty knowing all that faith entails. God uses Abraham's faith as an example of the type of faith required for salvation.

God's command to sacrifice Isaac was to provide an example of absolute obedience. After God gave the command, *early the next morning Abraham got up and loaded his donkey* and headed out with his son and the wood for a burnt offering (see Genesis 22:3). There was no delay, no questioning, no arguing. Just simple obedience, which brought a blessing (verses 15–18).

God's command to sacrifice Isaac was to reveal God as Jehovah-Jireh. On the way up the mountain to the place of sacrifice, Isaac inquired as to the animal to be sacrificed, and his father said, *God himself will provide the lamb for the burnt offering, my son* (see Genesis 22:8). After God's provision of a ram to take Isaac's place on the altar, *Abraham called that place The Lord Will Provide* (verse 14). Thus, we have another character-revealing name of God: Yahweh-Jireh.

How did Abraham know that God will provide a lamb (see Genesis 22:8)? Abraham knew that God would provide Himself with a lamb because, after years of having an immature faith, Abraham grew to fully trust that what God says He will do, He will do.

The author of Hebrews tells us what Abraham was thinking—how he could be willing to kill his son, and how he could know that God will provide Himself a lamb. When God told Abraham to sacrifice his son Isaac, Abraham considered that God was able to raise people from the dead (see Hebrews 11:19). God had promised Abraham that Isaac would be the covenant son, and that from Isaac God would raise up a mighty nation in fulfillment of the promises God had made to Abraham. God had already miraculously kept His promises—that Isaac was even born was a miracle in itself. Abraham had learned that God is faithful. At first, Abraham simply exercised faith (see Genesis 15:6), and God counted that to Abraham as righteousness (as He does with us when we believe in Him). But part of growing in our relationship with God is increasing in confidence that He is able and willing to accomplish what He has said. Because Abraham had seen God's faithfulness, when this uncharacteristic request of human sacrifice was made, Abraham trusted God that He knew what He was doing. Abraham knew that, even despite this strange and awful request, God would provide, and God would keep His word.

Before Abraham could bring the knife down to strike his son, the angel or messenger of the Lord called out to Him from Heaven acknowledging that Abraham had passed the test and should not kill Isaac (see Genesis 22:11–12). Of course, God never intended that Abraham would kill Isaac. He simply wanted to show Abraham that, no matter how impossible the circumstances, Abraham could trust God. As Abraham looked up, he saw a ram caught in a thicket nearby and offered the ram as a sacrifice instead of Isaac (see Genesis 22:13).

While Abraham's weakness of faith is chronicled in Genesis 18—21, God did not reject him or punish him for that immaturity. God did, however, provide him opportunities to grow and then puts him to the test so he can demonstrate that growth. Abraham learned that God is faithful, and even when we are unsure of how God is going to keep His word, we can be certain that He is faithful and that He will keep His word.

You don't ever have to be sick again. God's best for you is to live in divine health every day. Now, go ahead—receive your healing!

You don't ever have to deal with sickness or disease again. No matter what your situation, you can learn how to get and keep your healing once and for all!—Kenneth Copeland

I remember the day of the surgery. My doctor said, I won't know what needs to come out until I'm in there. I had to agree to an exploratory surgery and give him permission to do what he felt was best. It wasn't that I put my trust in him, I'd put my trust in God and made the choice to rest in Him and His promises. Despite the potential of waking from that surgery with a full hysterectomy I decided to rest because God knew what was best for me.

Remember when I said God said I'd have children? God never said how, I'd always assumed it would be children born of my womb, but what if it wasn't? Either way I had to rest on His Word.

I remember waking up in recovery, the first question I asked was, *What happened?* My mom told me the doctor only removed a cyst. Although this story is not over (it won't be until God fulfills His promise of motherhood to me) you've been equipped with enough wisdom to overcome sickness and break free from the spirit of unrest.

Steps to Overcome Sickness
1. Stand on the Word of God (see Psalm 103:2-3)
2. Don't let symptoms talk to you (see Romans 4:19)
3. Let go of doubt (see Matthew 13:58)
4. Cast your cares on the Lord (see 1 Peter 5:7)
5. Confess and possess (see Mark 11:23)
6. Never let go (see Hebrews 10:23)

Credit: https://blog.kcm.org/receive-keep-healing/

A Prayer to Overcome Sickness

Heavenly Father, I ask You now in the Name Jesus to release Your healing virtue, Your miracle virtue into my body in the Name of Jesus, release Your healing anointing, Your miracle anointing into my body, from the top of my head to the soles of my feet in the Name of Jesus. Heavenly Father, I ask You to make me whole, make me whole, Lord, in the Name of Jesus. Father, I ask You to restore every organ, every cell, every gland, every muscle, every ligament, every bone in my body and bring everything in total alignment, complete alignment, the way You created me, in the Name of Jesus.

Heavenly Father, I apply the Blood of Jesus over every organ, every cell, every gland, every muscle, every ligament, every bone in my body whether there is any disease, infection, virus, abnormal cells, radical cells, infirmity, or affliction of any kind in the Name of Jesus. Heavenly Father, I ask You to put a hedge of protection around me in the Name of Jesus. Heavenly Father, I apply the Blood of Jesus Christ over myself from the top of my head to the soles of my feet.

Heavenly Father, in the Name of the Lord, Jesus, I ask You to fill me with Your Holy Spirit; with all the fruits of Your Holy Spirit; Your love, Your joy, Your peace, Your patience, Your kindness, Your gentleness, Your faithfulness, and Your self-control, in the Name of Jesus. Heavenly Father, I thank You that You sent Your Son, Jesus, to the cross for me to take all my sicknesses, afflictions, infirmities, inflammations, infections, virus, and abnormal cells, etc. to the cross with Him. I ask You to do all of these things according to John 14:14; and Heavenly Father, I ask You to give me Divine healing, Divine health, the manifestation of Divine healing and Divine health, in the Name of the Lord Jesus; according to John 16:23.

Heavenly Father, according to Your Word "You are not a respecter of persons." I receive my healing, in Jesus' Holy Name. I forbid the enemy from trying to steal my healing. I bind my mind with the mind of Christ. I bring every thought captive to the obedience of Jesus Christ. Heavenly Father, fill me overflowing with Your Holy Spirit. In Jesus' Name I thank You for healing me. Amen!

Declarations to Overcome Sickness

I am convinced and sure that He who began a good work in me will continue until the day of Jesus Christ, developing and perfecting and bringing it to full completion in me. (see Philippians 1:6)

The thief comes only to steal and kill and destroy. You came, Lord, that I may have and enjoy life, and have it in abundance (to the full, till it overflows) (see John 10:10).

You, Lord, have taken my griefs (sicknesses, weaknesses, and distresses) and carried my sorrows and pains. You were wounded for my transgressions, bruised for my guilt and iniquities; the chastisement needed for my peace and well-being was upon You, Jesus, and by Your stripes I am healed and made whole (see Isaiah 53:4-5).

I gratefully praise You, Lord and do not forget all Your benefits. You forgive all my iniquities and heal all my diseases. You redeem my life from the pit and corruption. You beautify, dignify, and crown me with lovingkindness and tender mercy. You satisfy my mouth with good things, so my youth is renewed like the eagle's (Psalm 103:2-5).

I attend to God's Word and submit to His sayings. I will keep them in my sight, and in the center of my heart. They are life to me, and healing to my whole body (Proverbs 4:20-22).

Because I have made You, Lord, my refuge, and the Most High my dwelling place, no evil shall befall me, nor any plague or calamity come near my house. Because I have set my love on You, Lord, therefore You deliver me. You set me securely on high because I have known Your Name. I call upon You, Lord, and You answer me. You, Father, are with me in trouble. You deliver and honor me. With long life You will satisfy me and show me Your salvation (see Psalm 91:9-10, and 14-16).

God has not given me a spirit of timidity and fear. He has given me a spirit of power and of love and of a calm and well-balanced mind, discipline, and self-control (see 2 Timothy 1:7).

You give power to me when I am faint and weary. In my weakness, You increase strength in me. I wait for You [expect, look for, and hope in You] and You renew my strength and power. I will lift up with wings of strength and rise as an eagle. I shall run and not be weary, I shall walk and not faint or become tired (see Isaiah 40:29, and 31).

Even though I have a physical body, I will not carry on warfare according to the flesh, using mere human weapons. The weapons of my warfare are not physical (weapons of flesh and blood), they are mighty before God for the overthrow and destruction of strongholds. I refute arguments and theories and reasonings and every proud and lofty thing that sets itself up against the true knowledge of God; and I lead every thought and purpose away captive into the obedience of Christ (see 2 Corinthians 10:3-5).

I will not fret or have anxiety about anything, but in every circumstance and in everything, by prayer and petition, with thanksgiving, continue to make my requests known to God. God's peace, which transcends all understanding, shall garrison and mount guard over my heart and mind in Christ Jesus (see Philippians 4:6-7).

Credit: https://www.kcm.org/real-help/healing/speak/10-healing-confessions-every-day

Chapter Six

Overcoming Ungratefulness: Breaking Free from the Spirit of Discontentment

Ephesians 5:19-21 says, *[19]Speak to one another in psalms and hymns and spiritual songs, [offering praise by] singing and making melody with your heart to the Lord; [20]always giving thanks to God the Father for all things, in the name of our Lord Jesus Christ; [21]being subject to one another out of reverence for Christ.*

Philippians 4:12 says, *[12]I know how to get along and live humbly [in difficult times], and I also know how to enjoy abundance and live in prosperity. In any and every circumstance I have learned the secret [of facing life], whether well-fed or going hungry, whether having an abundance or being in need.* Paul could get along happily because he could see life from God's point of view. He focused on what he was supposed to do, not what he felt he should have. Paul had his priorities straight, and he was grateful for everything God had given him. Paul had detached himself from the nonessentials so that he could concentrate on the eternal.

Often the desire for more or better is really a longing to fill an empty place in a person's life. Merriam-Webster defines the word grateful as feeling or showing thanks or appreciation of benefits received. Being grateful is a by-product of contentment and I believe that is what Paul was speaking about in Philippians 4. The key to breaking free from discontentment and overcoming ungratefulness is realizing that everything we need can be found in Jesus, not in the people, places, and things of this world. Jesus is the One who can fill that empty place in your life. We will take a deeper look at Philippians 4 later in this chapter, but first, here are some definitions you should know:

Ungrateful—not feeling or showing gratitude.

Jealousy—feeling resentment against someone because of that person's success, and advantages.

Resentment—the feeling of being displeased or indignation at some act, remark, or person.

Envy—a feeling of discontent or covetousness about another's advantages, success, possessions etc.

Covetous—inordinately or wrong; desirous of wealth or possessions; greedy.

Inordinate—not within proper or reasonable limits.
Discontentment—lack of satisfaction with ones 'possessions, status, or situation.

All the above defined words are married to each other and when combined they equal one big gumbo called discontentment which stems from ungratefulness. Often, we set our hearts and our minds on the wrong things. We spend our entire lives in the pursuit of these things, these worldly things, these temporary things and never reach the contentment that we are seeking because nothing in this world can provide that. Due to this lifelong pursuit, some of us end up discontent, unhappy and ungrateful of the things we do have and have done. This is just not the way that God ordained for us to live but the lust of the eye is the problem.

First John 2:15-16 tells us, *¹⁵Do not love the world [of sin that opposes God and His precepts], nor the things that are in the world. If anyone loves the world, the love of the Father is not in him. ¹⁶For all that is in the world—the lust and sensual craving of the flesh and the lust and longing of the eyes and the boastful pride of life [pretentious confidence in one's resources or in the stability of earthly things]—these do not come from the Father but are from the world.*

Some people think that worldliness is limited to external behavior—the people we associate with, the places we go, the activities we enjoy. Worldliness is also internal because it begins in the heart and is characterized by three attitudes: (1) the lust of the flesh—preoccupation with gratifying physical desires; (2) the lust of the eyes—craving and accumulating things, bowing to the god of materialism; and (3) the pride of life—obsession with one's status or importance. When the serpent tempted Eve, he tempted her in these areas. Also, when the devil tempted Jesus in the wilderness, these were his three areas of attack (see Matthew 4:1-11).

By contrast, God values self-control, a spirit of generosity, and a commitment to humble service. It is possible to give the impression of avoiding worldly pleasures while still harboring worldly attitudes in one's heart. It is also possible, like Jesus, to love sinners and spend time with them while maintaining a commitment to the values of God's kingdom. What values are most important to you? Do your actions reflect the world's values or God's values? We need a Holy perspective change to overcome discontentment and ungratefulness, which is how I overcame it. Let me tell you about it.

For as far back as I can remember I have either always wanted what someone else had or wondered why it seems like bad people were always doing better than me. I specifically remember in middle school when I started to care about how I dressed; wondering why I had parents that couldn't afford to purchase name brand clothing. I was a good kid, I got good grades, avoided trouble and I followed direction at home and school. Somehow, the kids who were constantly getting in trouble at school by getting suspended always seemed to have on the latest fashions and they were popular because of it.

This drove me crazy in my adolescence. I was so ungrateful of what I had because even though I had the best that my parents could offer, it still wasn't good enough in my mind. I still remember the day I got my first brand new pair of name brand shoes; it was a white pair of Reeboks. I walked into that school building feeling like a million bucks. It is amazing how at such a young age I was already caught up in the things of this world. That seed only grew as I got older and entered adulthood.

As an adult, it got worse and more expensive. For me, it was cars, car accessories, and electronics. I liked big trucks, big rims, and customizations. I had a Ford Expedition that had 20-inch rims with spinners, custom lights, custom grill, top of the line stereo system and more. Her name was L-Boogie and that truck was my pride and joy and it made me feel like I had achieved something in life. I would also buy the latest electronics. Every few months I had something new or different, especially cell phones. When a new one came out, I had to get it the release day. I was so caught up in material (temporary) things that I wasn't paying much attention to the eternal things. I kept seeking more and more and I kept feeling ungrateful every time I got something new because I was trying to fill a void in my life that could only be filled by God. This vicious cycle ultimately left me feeling jealous & envious of others who seemed so happy with their things, resentful that my things were not producing the same effect, covetous because I wanted what they had and inordinate because I was simply out of order with God.

I was busy wasting time pursuing the things of this world when I should have been pursuing the things of my Heavenly Father. It wasn't until I started losing things that I began to realize how I was idolizing them. I was in a car accident and my beloved truck was totaled, every time I would get a new phone or electronic, something would go wrong with it, or I would drop or break it beyond repair. I couldn't figure out what the problem was, I was so mad, but then one day I was listening to a sermon and the preacher was talking about modern day idols. Boy did I receive a spiritual whipping that day. I learned everything I thought was important and gave me status, fame or popularity really wasn't important, hence the reason for my discontent.

All this time I had spent feeling ungrateful and discontent because I didn't have this or that, I had neglected to see how truly blessed I was. Despite me not pursuing the things of God, His hand was still upon my life. He woke me up every morning. I had both of my parents; they were still alive and married. I had a roof over my head, food on my table and clothes on my back. This began to help me focus on the things that matter in life. Moreover, it led me to begin seeking God about how I could find true contentment, like Paul, no matter what.

Paul gives us the standard for contentment and gratefulness in Philippians 4:11-13, where he says, *11Not that I speak from [any personal] need, for I have learned to be content [and self-sufficient through Christ, satisfied to the point where I am not disturbed or uneasy] regardless of my circumstances. 12I know how to get along and live humbly [in difficult times], and I also know how to enjoy abundance and live in prosperity. In any and every circumstance I have learned the secret [of facing life], whether well-fed or going hungry, whether having an abundance or being in need. 13I can do all things [which He has called me to do] through Him who strengthens and empowers me [to fulfill His purpose—I am self-sufficient in Christ's sufficiency; I am ready for anything and equal to anything through Him who infuses me with inner strength and confident peace.]*

Are you really content in any circumstance? Paul knew how to be content whether he had plenty or whether he was in need. The secret was drawing on Christ's power for strength. Do you have great needs, or are you discontented because you don't have what you want? Learn to rely on God's' promises and Christ's' power to help you be content. If you always want more, ask God to remove that desire and teach you contentment in every circumstance. He will supply all your needs, but in a way that He knows is best for you! Paul is driving home the point that nothing externally can bring us any kind of contentment, not clothes, shoes, electronics, cars, houses, people, places, or things.

The desire for more is really a longing to fill an empty place in a person's life. To what are you drawn when you feel empty inside? How can you find true contentment? The answer lies in your perspective, priorities, and source of power.

Our contentment is found within, through Jesus Christ when we accept Him into our lives and follow Him and not the things of this world. When we look around in this world, we can quickly begin to compare our lives to the lives of others. They look happy and successful, and we begin to attribute that to the things they have, and we begin to think *I need what they have*. This is our first problem. We think we need something when really; we want it and there is a big difference between a need and a want. The solution is learning to rely on God's' promises. God has promised to provide for each one of our needs in life. God is not a man that He would lie. He promised, and He will keep His promise. All you need is Him! Stop peeking through others' windows, you don't need what they have because what God has for you is for you!

Philippians 4:19 says, *[19]And my God will liberally supply (fill until full) your every need according to His riches in glory in Christ Jesus.* We can trust that God will always meet our needs. Whatever we need on earth He will always supply, even if it is the courage to face death, as Paul did. Whatever we need He will supply. We must remember, however, the difference between our wants and our needs. Most people want to feel good and avoid discomfort or pain. We may not get all that we want. But trusting in Christ, our attitudes and appetites can change from wanting everything to accepting His provision and power to live for Him.

Matthew 6:33 says, *³³But first and most importantly seek (aim at, strive after) His kingdom and His righteousness [His way of doing and being right—the attitude and character of God], and all these things will be given to you also.* I want to stop and caution you not to use God as a personal ATM. Yes, it is God's desire to bless us and see His children be prosperous in the Earth, however, it is also God's desire for us to have a true and genuine relationship with Him and not only come to Him when we want or need something. God doesn't always give us what we want, BUT HE ALWAYS gives us what we need. In His timing, not ours!

To *seek first His kingdom and His righteousness* means to turn to God first for help, to fill your thoughts with His desires, to take His character for your pattern, and to serve and obey Him in everything. What is important to you? People, objects, goals, and other desires all compete for priority. Any of these can quickly bump God out of first place if you don't actively choose to give Him first place in every area of your life.

Putting God first, seeking God first, relying fully on God for everything and having a true and genuine relationship with God will nullify the spirit of discontentment and ungratefulness. When you change your perspective and begin to view people, places, and things through the lens of the Word of God, you will begin to see that true wealth is not measured by achievements or possessions. True wealth is measured by contentment in God and righteous living.

First Timothy 6:6 says, *⁶But godliness actually is a source of great gain when accompanied by contentment [that contentment which comes from a sense of inner confidence based on the sufficiency of God]*. This statement is the key to breaking free from discontent—spiritual growth and personal fulfillment. We should honor God and center our desires on Him, and we should be content with what God is doing in our lives.

Overcoming discontentment and ungratefulness involves refocusing your perspective from the things of this world to the things of God. God will give you an inner peace and joy that nothing in this world will ever be able to replace! If I lost everything in this life but I still had Jesus, I would still be content. Would you? We can take our example from Job. He literally lost everything, BUT he said of God, *Though He slays me, yet will I trust Him!* (Job 13:15) My God, to have the perspective of Job! You can be content in Christ; you can overcome discontentment and ungratefulness by replacing everything you think you need in this life with Christ. Selah!

Steps to Overcome Ungratefulness

1. Remember never to forget (see Psalm 103:2; and Luke 17:11-19).
2. Do not major in your troubles (see Romans 8:28).
3. Think of how much better you are (see Hebrews 13:5).
4. Count your blessings (see 1 Timothy 6:6-8; and Ephesians 1:3).
5. Express your gratitude (see Psalms 107:1-8; and 116:12)
6. Do not take common things for granted (see 1 Thessalonians 5:18).
7. Do away with complaining (see Numbers 14:1-2; and Philippians 2:14)
8. We are a recipient and should never forget the gift (see James 1:17).

A Prayer to Overcome Ungratefulness

Father, You are my Shepherd and I should not be in want, but so often I struggle to be content and do want; forgetting that You have graciously provided me with every spiritual blessing in Christ and everything I need for life and godliness.

Thank You for often not giving me what I want because my desires would draw my heart from being satisfied in You. Help me to be content in You with what You have given me and to not be focused on what my flesh wants, or the world tells me I should have.

Protect me from coveting possessions or people, talent or influence, relationships, or prestige. Keep my heart from being anxious for what I don't have and make me thankful for the numerous gifts that You have already given.

According to Your Word and steadfast love, fill me with the joy and satisfaction of contentment in Christ. Help me learn to be content in any situation like Paul and to quickly reject the idolatry that dwells beneath the surface of my coveting.

I ask you to continually bring to mind Your faithful provision for all my needs, that Christ died for the sin of coveting, that in Christ I am free to be content and live righteously, and that godliness with contentment is greater gain than pleasing my flesh.

And may I be humbled and changed by the ultimate example of contentment; of Christ becoming poor in order that I could become rich and being content to go to the Cross to fulfill the Father's will to rescue a people for Himself who can be free from discontent and zealous for good works. In Jesus Name. Amen.

Credit: https://www.kevinhalloran.net/a-prayer-for-contentment/

Declarations to Overcome Ungratefulness

What I have is enough.

The time I have is enough.

The people around me are enough.

I am enough.

God is enough.

> Credit: https://marcalanschelske.com/guest-speaker/overview-gratitude

Chapter Seven

Overcoming Shame: Breaking Free from the Spirit of Humiliation

Shame: a painful feeling or humiliation or distress caused by the consciousness of wrong or foolish behavior

Humiliation: the action of humiliating someone or the state of being humiliated:

Shalom: peace

> *I am convinced and confident of this very thing, that He who has begun a good work in you will [continue to] perfect and complete it until the day of Christ Jesus [the time of His return].*
> Philippians 1:6

Do you sometimes feel as though you aren't making progress in your spiritual life? When God starts a project, He completes it! As with the Philippians, God will help you grow in grace until He has completed His work in your life. When you are discouraged, remember that God won't give up on you. He promises to finish the work He has begun. When you feel incomplete, unfinished, or distressed by your shortcomings, remember God's promise and provision. Don't let your present condition rob you of the joy of knowing Christ or keep you from growing close to Him.

In the eighth grade, I read a book called *The Scarlet Letter*. In short, the book is about a married woman who has an affair that produces a child. In the town where she lives, she is publicly shamed for her indiscretions and is forced to wear a scarlet, gold-embroidered patch of cloth in the shape of an *A*.

If you are like me, this story sounds familiar to you. It sounds familiar because many of us carry shame around in our hearts and minds in the same way the character in this story did on her chest. There are things we have said and things we have done that we carry around like a bright red ketchup stain on a crisp white shirt. It wasn't until I was having a conversation with one of my dear covenant sisters that I realized I was still carrying the sin stain from things I had done in my past.

As you have read in an earlier chapter, between the ages of five and nine years of age, I was raped by one male and molested by five males, and one female. I was so young I didn't really understand what was happening or going on, but these series of unfortunate events set in motion God's plan and purpose for my life. Statistics show childhood sexual trauma is associated with posttraumatic stress disorder (PTSD), depression, suicide, alcohol problems, and eating disorders. Survivors may also experience low sexual interest and relationship difficulties or engage in high-risk sexual behaviors and extreme coping strategies.

For years I believed I was on the other end of the spectrum with no desire for sex or intimacy, but I kept finding myself in these situationships with men, where I'd draw a line which stopped just short of sexual intercourse. Psychologically I felt like I was damaged goods, so any attention I could get from a male was good enough for me, even if it was just temporary as a means for him to attempt to *get some*. Emotionally I was confused. I knew what I was doing was wrong but if I wasn't having sexual intercourse or going *all the way*, I was justified in my acts, because premarital sex was a sin. Spiritually I was dead. I knew of God and had seen Him work in various ways throughout my life, but I did not know Him or have an active intimate relationship with Him. I'd, in a sense, turned my back on Him because I was trying to fill a void only He could fill. Physically I was not engaged or aroused and often wondered why I kept allowing myself to be in these situations in the first place just to try to get a boyfriend or please a man.

So, I wasn't promiscuous in the sense of having multiple sexual partners, but I was promiscuous in the sense allowing myself to be prematurely exposed to things I had no business being engaged in. I exposed myself to sinful acts which opened doors in my heart and mind that should never have been opened. I exposed myself to men who had not paid the price of admission called marriage, and I was opening doors to demons.

> I exposed myself to men who had not paid the price of admission called marriage.

As a result of my actions, even after I came to know Christ and began a personal relationship with Him shame followed me around like a nagging younger sibling; but I never acknowledged it or even knew it was there. Instead, it manifested in a variety of different ways, like in my confidence, my self-esteem, my body image, and the value that I placed on myself.

I knew the sins I'd committed were wrong, and I also knew my sins were covered by the Blood of Christ, but the disconnect came in me not actively believing and applying what I knew. Not only that, but secrecy also prohibited me from really addressing firstly the rape and molestation, and secondly the aftereffects of experiencing sexual trauma. For years I kept the rape and molestation a secret. It happened when I was five, it was exposed when I was 21 and I didn't seek the help of a professional Christian counselor until I was 29. That's a total of 24 years I was held captive to a skewed view of sex, men, and myself. That's more than 15 years of walking around wearing a scarlet letter *A* that only I could see, but I felt like everyone could see it and my indiscretions. That's more than 15 years of shame and humiliation, which needed to be addressed and dealt with, so I could arrive at this place to be able to share my story with you and help you begin washing the stain of shame from your heart, mind, and soul.

I made it through high school without ever having a boyfriend, *hooking up*, kissing, or having sex. I went to school in Pennsylvania at LaRoche College for my freshmen year of college. I was excited about school because I believed the myth that you find your spouse, date while in college and then get married after you graduate. I always wanted a boyfriend. It seemed like everyone was hooking up and dating but me, so I decided to join some online sites. On one of these sites, I met a guy who was in school in Chester Pennsylvania, which was about three hours from where I went to school. We talked for a little bit online, and he convinced me to come to see him. I had a car in college, so I drove the three hours to see him. He was a Resident Assistant, so he had his own room. I got there and he asked if I was hungry. I said yes, so we left in my car to go eat. I was just following his directions assuming we were going to a restaurant. We went to Wawa, and he got us subs, then we went back to the room where we ate the subs.

As soon as he finished his sub. He leaned over to kiss me. I closed my lips tight and all I felt was teeth and his tongue. He got up, cut the lights off and told me to get into bed. I pulled my clothes off and got in the bed. He got on top of me and started humping away. It dawned on me that he didn't know what he was doing. I just laid there making a couple noises when he made noises. I was completely fine with him not knowing he was not actually having sex with me. I was watching the clock and after five minutes he was done. He sat on the side of the bed and said, "Oh my God! That was my first time!" I didn't say anything. I asked where the showers were. I went and showered and came back and he was in the bed. He said I could sleep on the couch. I didn't sleep. I was awake all-night listening to him snore. That night I felt the same way I felt the night my uncle's girlfriend's son tried to rape me. I felt dirty and dumb. The next morning, he walked me out to my car and tried to kiss me again. I closed my lips tight. He said he had a good time. I just got in the car and left. I had to drive three hours back to campus feeling like a dummy. I lied to my roommates about what happened. I had become a good liar about not being a virgin and about having a fake boyfriend. I wanted to fit in and not be the only one not sharing stories or talking about a boyfriend. I felt stupid for that too. We did talk a few times after that night until he told me he had a girlfriend, and we couldn't talk anymore. Again, I felt stupid.

When I was 22, I moved back to Maryland. I joined this dating site called College Luv. I started talking to this guy who was 6'7, and from Nigeria. We talked online for about three weeks then decided to go out on a date. This was the first real date I had ever been on! I was so excited. We went to the movies, saw *Matrix Revolutions*, and got something to eat at one of the restaurants there afterwards. He paid for everything, put his arm around me in the movies and even kissed me on my neck goodnight when we were leaving. I still remember that kiss on the neck, that's when I discovered my neck was a hot zone for me. He called me and we talked for another week or two before he invited me over to his house for dinner. This was the only guy that had ever shown me real interest and he was tall, so I was all in of course. I went to his house, and he cooked dinner. This was the guy (from chapter two) I caught the cramps with. The next day he sent me an email saying that he wanted me to be his girlfriend, but he would have to have sex with me first before he knew for sure. I never responded and never heard from him again.

Right after him was the man I thought I was going to marry. I think I was in strong like with him. We talked for a year. He showed me attention and asked about me, but he never wanted to call me his girlfriend. We were friends with partial benefits. On October 4, 2005, I asked him what we were. He said he loved me, but we were just friends. Soon after he stopped calling, we stopped talking and he was very distant. I asked what was up and he said that he wanted to see what other American girls were like. He told me that I was a bet between him and his brother. I was humiliated and felt dumb all over again. There were so many signs that I wasn't the only one and that he really wasn't into me like I was him, all of which I ignored because he was handsome, tall, and showed interest in me. He was 6'5. Again, I felt dumb, stupid, humiliated, and rejected. I felt if I would've had sexual intercourse with him instead of only going so far, he would have made me his girlfriend or wife.

Over the next couple months, I went on a few dates with guys from different dating sites, some of them got small pieces of me and were allowed some access, but they were not entitled to all of me. They were first dates only. I met a guy on Black People Meet once. He was Jamaican. We talked for a while. Then decided to go out on a date. We met in Silver Spring. We were supposed to see a movie and have dinner. We talked for a bit on the way to the restaurant. Once we got there, he got a phone call and said he had to go. He ran out of the restaurant and left me there. He literally ran to his car. I watched him. I sat there yet again feeling like a fool. I never heard his phone ring. And the call came shortly after I told him I was waiting until marriage to have sex. Again, I just felt dumb and rejected. I later found out he was just in DC for work and had a wife and kids at home in Boston.

Next, was a guy from my mom's job. I thought things would go better with him because we met in person. We talked via AIM messenger for a while and then went out on a date. He was cute, from Ethiopia, and he had a good job. He wanted to take me to an Ethiopian restaurant. There was one in Silver Spring. We met and saw the movie *I Am Legend* first then went to the restaurant. By this time, I had rededicated my life to Christ and was the youth leader at my church. I hadn't been out since the married Jamaican which had been a while and since I had rededicated my life, I said I wouldn't put myself in any compromising positions again. So, I told myself I wouldn't go to his house if he invited me that night.

Low and behold after the movie and dinner he invited me to his house and like a dummy I went. We sat on the couch and looked through photo albums of his family. He offered me something to drink. I asked for water, and he went to the kitchen and came back with an erection. I was confused about what happened in the kitchen, but I knew it was time to go at that point. He sat back down. Grabbed my face and pulled me in to kiss him. I closed my lips tight and all I felt was teeth and tongue. He was very forceful. At this point I panicked, pulled away and got up to leave. He grabbed me by both arms and pulled me back to him to try to kiss me again. I told him to let go of me, and I guess it was either my tone or my face that convinced him to let me go. I left and felt so dumb on the way home, thinking about the fact that I could have been raped or anything could have happened all because I went back to his house, and I shouldn't have.

The next day he messaged me and apologized and asked me not to tell my mother. He said he never had sex and thought that was what girls liked. We didn't talk anymore until I had to take a cake up to my mom's job. He pulled me out in the hall and apologized again. I said it was all good and left.

Next was a family friend's nephew who was here visiting from out of town. We texted the whole week he was in town. The day before he left was October 31. I had gone over to the family friend's house. She left to go to the grocery store. The week we were texting was all dirty texts, mostly from him and of him asking me to send him nude pictures. I never sent any although he sent me some of himself. He told me all that he would do to me including oral sex which I had never experienced. He said he would perform oral sex on me, so I was all for it. That day after my friend left we went and got something to eat. Then we came back. He went upstairs. I was downstairs. He texted me and asked me to come upstairs. I went upstairs and walked into the bedroom, and he had his shirt off, and he had an erection. I said I didn't want to have sex, but I did want him to do what he said he was going to do. He said he would but instead all he wanted was sex. That wasn't the agreement, so I left. Since him, I have never tried anything else or put myself in a compromising position ever again.

I did meet a guy at church. We went on a couple dates, and he offered to perform oral sex on me as well. We went to a hotel to do the deed, but I couldn't walk in, I was literally stuck at the entrance of the hotel. It was like there was a force field preventing me from walking to it. It was a weird experience. Now, I like to think God had angels there blocking me. Anyway, other than a kiss on the neck nothing really happened between us. I found out he was living with a woman who he said he wasn't intimate with, but he really was. I didn't want to be a side chick, so I cut that off. And he had gotten mad with me one night when I wouldn't come pick him up in the middle of the night, so we never talked again, and he stopped coming to church.

I went on one other date with a guy I met at Panera Bread. He was a Haitian. We went on a date and that was it. I haven't dated, been in a relationship or been with a guy in any way since then. That was 17 years ago.

There is a lot of guilt and shame wrapped up in those stories. Here is the blessing of it all. God washed the stain of my sin and removed my scarlet letter in less than 24 hours. How? I exposed the secret, recognized the shame and how it was manifesting in my life, and resolved within myself to share my story. No, I am not saying it will happen this fast for everyone, but the point I want to drive home is that God is faithful to complete the good work He began in us before the foundation of the earth.

While the earth was still formless and empty, and darkness was over the surface of the deep, and the Spirit of God was hovering over the waters, you were but a thought in God's mind. You see, God knew us, He already knew, the mistakes you would make, He already knew the sins you'd commit, He already knew the foolish behavior you'd engage in, and He already made room in the plan of your life to cover those sins and mistakes. God's grace covers a multitude of sins. It is not God's desire for us to live in sorrow and shame. It is His desire that we live in peace and harmony with Him. It is His desire that we commune in intimate covenant and relationship with Him. But it is impossible for us to do that if we are living in shame, tormented by the thoughts we allow the enemy to place in our minds about our past.

God has many names but the one that applies here is Jehovah Shalom. Jehovah means Lord, Holiness, Truth revealer, righteousness, and redemption. The word shalom is a harmony or reconciliation of relationship based upon the completion of a transaction, the payment of a debt, the giving of satisfaction. God wants to expose the shame we carry (Truth Revealer), put us in right standing with Him (righteousness) and redeem us from our wrong, sinful, foolish behaviors (redemption). God sent His Son Jesus as the payment of the debt we created through sin (shalom). God used Jesus to reconcile us back to Himself.

The key to breaking the power of shame is the superior power of faith in the work of Christ and the promises of Christ. Shame pronounces us guilty and deficient. Jesus pronounces us guiltless and promises that His grace will be sufficient for us in all our weaknesses. Second Corinthians 12:9–10 says, *⁹"My grace is sufficient for you [My lovingkindness and My mercy are more than enough—always available—regardless of the situation]; for [My] power is being perfected [and is completed and shows itself most effectively] in [your] weakness." Therefore, I will all the more gladly boast in my weaknesses, so that the power of Christ [may completely enfold me and] may dwell in me. ¹⁰So I am well pleased with weaknesses, with insults, with distresses, with persecutions, and with difficulties, for the sake of Christ; for when I am weak [in human strength], then I am strong [truly able, truly powerful, truly drawing from God's strength]."* As we trust Jesus as our righteousness and our provider of everything we need, shame will lose its power over us and God's peace will become obtainable.

God revealed five truths about His peace:
1. Jesus provided our peace for us by His own death.
Romans 5:1 says, *Therefore, since we have been justified [that is, acquitted of sin, declared blameless before God] by faith, [let us grasp the fact that] we have peace with God [and the joy of*

reconciliation with Him] through our Lord Jesus Christ (the Messiah, the Anointed). We now have peace with God, which may differ from peaceful feelings such as tranquility and calmness. Peace with God means that we have been reconciled with Him. There is no more hostility because of us, and no shame or sin is blocking our relationship with Him. Peace with God is possible only because Jesus paid the price for our sins through His death on the Cross.

Romans 5:9-10 says, *9Therefore, since we have now been justified [declared free of the guilt of sin] by His blood, [how much more certain is it that] we will be saved from the wrath of God through Him. 10For if while we were enemies we were reconciled to God through the death of His Son, it is much more certain, having been reconciled, that we will be saved [from the consequences of sin] by His life [that is, we will be saved because Christ lives today]*. The love that caused Christ to die is the same love that sends the Holy Spirit to live in us and guide us every day. The power that raised Christ from the dead is the same power that saved you and is available to you in your daily life. It's this same power that trumps shame if you allow it to. Be assured that, having begun a life with Christ, you have a reserve of power and love to call on each day, for help to meet every challenge or trial. You can pray for God's power and love as you need it.

2. The measure of peace that we have in Him is determined by our sanctification and trust in Him.

> Do you want to worry less? Then pray more!

Philippians 4:6-7 says *⁶Do not be anxious or worried about anything, but in everything [every circumstance and situation] by prayer and petition with thanksgiving, continue to make your [specific] requests known to God. ⁷And the peace of God [that peace which reassures the heart, that peace] which transcends all understanding, [that peace which] stands guard over your hearts and your minds in Christ Jesus [is yours]."* I was not satisfied with myself because of the shame which trickled down into me not being satisfied with God or even trusting Him. I was anxious all the time but imagine being anxious for nothing! It seems like an impossibility. We may have worries on the job, in our homes, or at school, but Paul's advice is to turn your worries into prayers. Do you want to worry less? Then pray more! Whenever you start to worry, stop, and pray.

3. God's peace is different from the world's peace.
John 14: 27 says, *Peace I leave with you; My [perfect] peace I give to you; not as the world gives do I give to you. Do not let your heart be troubled, nor let it be afraid. [Let My perfect peace calm you in every circumstance and give you courage and strength for every challenge.]* The result of the Holy Spirit's work in our

lives is deep and lasting peace. Unlike worldly peace, which is usually defined as the absence of conflict, this peace is confident assurance in any circumstance, and with Christ's peace, we have no need to fear the past, present or future. If your life is full of shame, allow the Holy Spirit to fill you with Christ's peace.

True peace is not found in positive thinking, in the absence of conflict, or in good feelings. It comes from knowing that God is in control. It comes from knowing that God already knew where you'd be right now. It comes from knowing nothing is a secret from Him and He loves you unconditionally anyway. He knows the dirty little nasty things you have done and what you thought were secret. God is El Roi, which means the God who sees. He knew it, He saw it, and He still loves every ounce of you, unconditionally. Our citizenship in Christ's kingdom is sure, our destiny is set, and we can have victory over shame. Let God's peace guard your heart against shame.

> He knows the dirty little nasty things you have done and what you thought were secret.

4. The peace of God comes through spiritual mindedness. Romans 8:6-8 says, *⁶Now the mind of the flesh is death [both now and forever—because it pursues sin]; but the mind of the Spirit is life and peace [the spiritual well-being that comes from walking with God—both now and forever]; ⁷the mind of the flesh*

[with its sinful pursuits] is actively hostile to God. It does not submit itself to God's law, since it cannot, ⁸and those who are in the flesh [living a life that caters to sinful appetites and impulses] cannot please God. Paul divides people into two categories—those who let themselves be controlled by their sinful natures, and those who follow the Holy Spirit. All of us would be in the first category if Jesus hadn't offered us a way out. Once we have said yes to Jesus, we will want to continue following Him, because His way brings life and peace. Daily we must consciously choose to center our lives on God. Use the Bible to discover God's guidelines, and then follow them. In every perplexing situation, ask yourself, *What would Jesus want me to do?* When the Holy Spirit points out what is right, do it eagerly. When the Holy Spirit points out shame and sin, like He did for me, begin taking steps to address it immediately.

5. Peace is part of the fruit of the Holy Spirit.
Galatians 5:22-24 says, *²²But the fruit of the Spirit [the result of His presence within us] is love [unselfish concern for others], joy, [inner] peace, patience [not the ability to wait, but how we act while waiting], kindness, goodness, faithfulness, ²³gentleness, self-control. Against such things there is no law. ²⁴And those who belong to Christ Jesus have crucified the [a]sinful nature together with its passions and appetites.* The fruit of the Spirit is the spontaneous work of the Holy Spirit in us. The Spirit produces these character traits that are found in Christ. They are by-

products of Christ's control—we can't obtain them by trying to get them without His help. If we want the fruit of the Spirit to grow in us, we must join our lives to His. We must know Him, love Him, remember Him, and imitate Him. As a result, we will fulfill the intended purpose of the law, to love God and our neighbors and we will live a life of peace, shame-free.

In conclusion, there is no peace besides that which can come by way of Christ. There is no other way.

Know Jesus, Know Peace. No Jesus.No Peace

When we have a relationship with God through His Son, Jesus; He becomes our Jehovah-Shalom—the One who brings the peace that passes all understanding and trumps all shame.

And so, let us pray:
- *That the Spirit would bring into conscious awareness the cause(s) of shame.* What specific incidents in one's past were the reason why one now feels shame? Ask the Spirit to bring light and insight into what happened, when, and by whom it was done. (use the space below to record what the Holy Spirit reveals):

_____
_____
_____

- *That the Spirit would awaken you to the realities of the Gospel; that the Spirit would strengthen your faith in the truth of all that God has done for us in Christ to secure for us the complete and comprehensive forgiveness of sins.*

- *That the Spirit would awaken you to who you are as an adopted child of God* (see Romans 8:15-16 and Galatians 4:4-7).

- *That the Spirit would break the stranglehold the enemy has exerted on you. Satan wants to undermine your intimacy with Christ by convincing you that he would never want fellowship with someone who has done the things you've done.* Satan wants to paralyze your usefulness to the church and to others by convincing you that you are an embarrassment and a reproach. Thus, we must pray that the Spirit would silence the voice of the enemy that has led you to believe that you are beyond the hope of God's love and forgiveness.

- *That the Spirit would indelibly imprint on your heart the deep and abiding conviction that God rejoices over you and sings over you in delight* (see Zephaniah 3:17).

- *That the Spirit would shine the light of truth into your heart and dispel the darkness of lies.*

- *That the Spirit would quicken your heart to feel the love of Christ* (see Ephesians 3:14-21).

- *That the Spirit would bring to mind any sins committed that led to bondage and shame humiliation.*

- *That the Spirit would enable you to repent honestly and openly and thoroughly.*

- *That the Spirit would enable you to openly confess your sins to others.*

Credit: https://www.crosswalk.com/faith/spiritual-life/how-the-holy-spirit-delivers-you-from-shame.html

Steps to Overcome Shame

1. Identify whether you're experiencing shame or guilt.
2. Confess any sin to God (see 1 John 1:8-9; and Acts 3:19).
3. Believe that God has forgiven you (see Isaiah 1:18; Hebrews 8:12; and Psalm 103:3).
4. Forgive yourself (see Matthew 6:14-15).
5. Confess your sin to someone you trust (see James 5:16).
6. Break the power of shame from the Enemy (see Luke 10:19).
7. Overcome shame by declaring God's Word (see Psalm 103:10-12; Romans 8:1; and Zephaniah 3:19).
8. Stop rehearsing the past (see 2 Corinthians 10:4-5; and Philippians 3:13-14)

Credit: https://www.funandholy.com/blog/howtoletgoofshame

A Prayer to Overcome Shame

God, I confess that I have sinned and what I did was wrong. I repent from my sin, and I ask for Your forgiveness. I surrender this guilt and sin to You Lord, and I thank You that I have been forgiven.

I thank You that You do not deal with me as my sins deserve. I thank You that you sent Jesus to die on the Cross for my sins, and that I am forgiven. I believe that I have been forgiven, and I release my shame to You. I choose to walk in the freedom that Jesus Christ died to give me.

I thank You that You've already forgiven me for my sins. Today, I choose to forgive myself for what I've done. If You have forgiven me Lord, I can forgive myself. I forgive myself, and I release any shame that I've been carrying.

I thank You for bringing people into my life that love and encourage me on this journey. Give me the courage to reach out and ask for help. Show me the people in my life that I can trust, and who will speak Your truth in love.

I thank You that You've given me authority over the enemy. I renounce and break any agreement that I've had with shame. I have been forgiven for my sins, and I renounce the lie that I need to feel ashamed of what I've done. I declare shame to leave in Jesus' name, and I declare that the power of shame has been broken in my life.

I hold every thought captive to the Word of God, and I reject these thoughts that aren't from You. I command the devil to leave me alone. Resist the devil and he must flee. I reject the lie that I'm not worthy to be forgiven in Jesus' name, and I command shame to leave. I have been forgiven for my past, and I am free from shame. In the strong name of Jesus I pray, Amen.

Credit: https://www.funandholy.com/blog/howtoletgoofshame

Declarations to Overcome Shame

I know and believe the love God has for me! It isn't just for other people—it is FOR ME right now, exactly where I am in my life. It is perfect and it is FOR ME.

I declare I am completely free of condemnation! Jesus does not condemn me—He wipes the slate clean and invites me to step even deeper into His heart.

I accept my righteous standing with God the Father! HIS righteousness has become MY righteousness! I am perfectly innocent in His sight. Jesus Himself stands before Father God speaking well of me.

Credit: https://btomovement.org/daily-devotional/declarations-for-conquering-shame

Chapter Eight
Free Indeed

What you will find on the other side of overcoming is FREEDOM!

John 8:36 (NKJV) says, *36Therefore if the Son makes you free, you shall be free indeed.* In John 8 Jesus exhorts His listeners that if they abide in His Word, they would be truly His disciples, they will know the truth, and that truth would make them free (see John 8:31-32). They were a bit surprised to hear that because, as they were descendants of Abraham, they thought they had never been enslaved (see John 8:33). Jesus then explained that, if a person is committing sin, that person is enslaved by sin, and slavery is not fitting for sons (see John 8:34-35). But if the Son—Jesus says, referring to Himself—makes us free, then we *are free indeed* (see John 8:36). He is the Son who remains forever, so what He determines shall stand. When He gives the recipe that we are *free indeed*, it is a reliable recipe because of who He is. The condition for becoming *free indeed* is that His hearers should abide (or dwell) in His Word. He later explains that keeping His Word results in eternal life (see John 8:52), and He challenges His hearers that they need to believe in Him (see John 8:46).

After expressing that there is no condemnation for those who are in Christ Jesus (see Romans 8:1), Paul adds that in Christ Jesus we have been set free from the law of sin and death (see Romans 8:2). Because of that new freedom, we are no longer in bondage to sinfulness, and now we can choose righteousness (see Romans 9:12–15). Peter adds a caution that we use this freedom not as an excuse for evil but that we use this freedom to walk in devoted service to God—as bondslaves (see 1 Peter 2:16).

Jesus came offering something very special, and if we take Him at His word then we are free indeed. He is *the truth* (see John 14:6), and He desires that we abide in Him and walk in Him. As He expresses in John 15:5, *⁵I am the vine; you are the branches. If you remain in me and I in you, you will bear much fruit; apart from me you can do nothing.* Jesus wants to set us free from the curse of sin, shame, and death. He gave His own life so that we could be *free indeed* and asks us simply to believe in Him.

The true freedom that Jesus gives is freedom (1) from the <u>penalty</u> of sin—there is no more condemnation for those in Him (see Romans 8:1), and no longer are we children of wrath (see Ephesians 2:1–3); (2) from the <u>power</u> of sin—no longer are we in bondage to sin, but now we can do righteousness; without faith it is impossible to please Him, but, with faith, we can please Him (see Hebrews 11:6); and one day we will be free (3) from the *presence* of sin—when our eternal life is fulfilled, we will be like Him and without sin (see Romans 8:28–30).

On the other side of overcoming to are free to live and your capacity can now be expanded. One of the reasons it's so important to understand that you are free from the bondage, penalty and guilt of sin is because it now increases your capacity. Jesus wants to increase your capacity to love, to have joy, to experience peace, to enjoy life, serve His people and advance His Kingdom.

He also wants to increase your capacity to have a relationship with your Heavenly Father. This can't happen if you are not free. You cannot have a vibrant, living, loving relationship with God or with anyone else for that matter, if you are holding on to the guilt and shame of your past. Jesus said in John 10:10, *¹⁰The thief comes only to steal and kill and destroy. I came that they may have and enjoy life, and have it in abundance [to the full, till it overflows].*

In contrast to the thief who takes life, Jesus gives life. The life He gives right now is abundantly richer and fuller. It is eternal, yet it begins immediately. Life in Christ is lived on a higher plane because of His overflowing forgiveness, love, and guidance. Have you taken Christ's offer of life?

If you remember in the garden when Adam and Eve sinned, they hid from God and their capacity for a relationship with God was hindered. When Jesus comes and sets you free you don't have to hide anymore. You can now enjoy a healthy relationship with your Heavenly Father and He encourages it. James 4:8 says, *⁸Come near to God and he will come near to you.* This is the essence of what Christ has freed you to. God wants close, intimate fellowship with you and the only way that happens is by Jesus freeing you. This allows you to build that relationship without fear or worry. You can enter God's presence with confidence because you know he wants you there and the hindrances have all been removed. This truly is living free.

On the other side of overcoming, you are free to serve, and your activity will not be hindered. Ephesians 2:10 says, *¹⁰For we are His workmanship [His own master work, a work of art], created in Christ Jesus [reborn from above—spiritually transformed, renewed, ready to be used] for good works, which God prepared [for us] beforehand [taking paths which He set], so that we would walk in them [living the good life which He prearranged and made ready for us].* We are God's workmanship (work of art, masterpiece). We become Christians through God's unmerited grace, not as a result of any effort, ability, intelligent choice, or act of service on our part. However, out of gratitude for this free gift, we will seek to help and serve others with kindness, love, and gentleness, and not merely to please ourselves. While no action or work we do can help us obtain favor, God's intention is that our salvation will result in acts of service. We are not saved merely for our own benefit but to serve Christ and build up the church.

Our salvation is something only God can do. It is His powerful, creative work in us. If God considers us His works of art, we dare not treat ourselves or others with disrespect or as inferior work. One of the other reasons Christ has freed you is because He has work for you to do. He has a plan for your life. However, it will be difficult to achieve this plan if you are running around with a guilty conscience. When you do this, you are always trying to prove yourself or win the approval of the person you are serving.

Let me lighten the load for you today. You are saved by grace. You live by grace. God will accomplish His plan in your life by grace. Christ frees you so that your activity doesn't flow out of some sense of trying to win God's approval. Your approval doesn't come because of what you do, but because of what Christ has already done. When you understand this, you are free to accomplish the plan God has for your life with no agenda, no ulterior motive but out of a heart motivated by love for Him.

Chapter Nine
Unquestionably Free

In the early church deliverance was a standard procedure to remove the demons that were still in a person after they became a follower of Jesus. These were left over from their pre-Christian days and unless removed would make the Christian life difficult to live often manifesting as sins or bad habits you have difficulty breaking as they are continually there influencing you to do them.

Christians cannot be possessed because The Holy Spirit's presence is placed in their spirit to mark them as belonging to Jesus, so demons cannot gain entry. But Jesus said that people have a house (which is their soul) and demons can inhabit that.

Matthew 12:43-45 says, *[43]Now when the unclean spirit has gone out of a man, it roams through waterless (dry, arid) places in search of rest, but it does not find it. [44]Then it says, 'I will return to my house from which I came.' And when it arrives, it finds the place unoccupied, swept, and put in order. [45]Then it goes and brings with it seven other spirits more wicked than itself, and they go in and make their home there. And the last condition of that man becomes worse than the first. So will it also be with this wicked generation.*

This is why we ask The Holy Spirit to fill the house (soul), so demons do not have a place to come back in and must persuade you to let them come back in. This is why holiness is so important in keeping them out.

This ministry of deliverance removes all Satan placed on a person while in bondage, in their mind and/or soul, when they belonged to his kingdom.

When you become a Christian, God may heal you and/or remove demons you picked up. They are removed from your Spirit because The Holy Spirit takes over it, but they may still be in your soul causing you problems.

Deliverance was a normal ministry to those becoming Christians in the early church but is ignored today because people do not realize demons can still inhabit the soul of Christians. Deliverance heals the spiritual damage Satan did to them, removes any demons in them and sometimes heals any physical damage related to the area being delivered in. It is a lordship decision which is why Jesus showed we should do deliverance using a lordship prayer rather than needlessly fighting demons.

It is based on James 4:7 which says: *So, submit to [the authority of] God. Resist the devil [stand firm against him] and he will flee from you.*

The delegation to remove the demons is found in Mark 16:17 which says: *These signs will accompany those who have believed: in My name they will cast out demons, they will speak in new tongues;...*

Note the use of the name of Jesus is to cast out demons and attack their works and not as an automatic conclusion to prayer. If you believe modern Bibles are the best translation, then you have a problem as you really cannot do deliverance using them. They imply this delegation was put in by men and not Jesus. They do this because the Greek codex they use to translate modern bibles does not have this verse in it. The problem is that it was in the original codex but was left out for some reason when they were published.

There are two principles in this method of deliverance:
1. Give what is being requested to be delivered to Him to be Lord of so Satan must fight Jesus for it or persuade you to give it back to Him
2. Tell Satan to go so He knows you do not want what he offers you.

This is the basis of a simple five step process.

The Pattern is as follows:

1. Give to Jesus to be Lord of what you want to be delivered from.
2. Check there is no unforgiveness or sin you do not want to give up.
3. Command Satan to leave in Jesus Name
4. In the Name of Jesus command healing and restoration in accordance with the Will of God
5. Ask the Holy Spirit to fill you with His Presence so that there is no place for demons to come back in.

The following is the prayer you will use to walk through deliverance (broken into five easy to understand steps).

All except steps three and four can be prayed silently in your heart. Steps three and four can be whispered, so only you, God, and Satan hear them being commanded. This prayer can be said without the need of another to be there so that only you and Jesus knows what is being prayed.

Step 1

Give to Jesus, quietly in your heart, anything that troubles you. You do not need to name the sins, just the area the sin or problem is in, for Jesus to be Lord of. All you need to do is to agree to give the following in your heart for Jesus to be Lord of. So, give to Jesus any:

- Moral weaknesses you have
- Sins you have trouble defeating.
- Loveless acts toward others
- Circumstances or events you are anxious or concerned/worried about
- Wrong emotions, habits, attitudes, values, or wrong coping mechanisms you have
- Wrong understanding, knowledge and learning, wrong worship, or attitudes to God
- Hurtful memories you have that cause you problems of any kind.
- Wrong relationships you have
- Betrothal (engagement) and social activities
- Marriage, family, and any problems in that area
- Employment
- Ministry
- Fear of Authority
- Fear of Failure
- All others fear.
- Any wrong agreements or contracts; whether you know you have made them.
- Past hurts, traumatic events and other events that have hurt you in ally way.
- Anything, in you or that you have done that is, not of Jesus or His Kingdom which He is not already Lord of. Whether or not you know they are there.

- Anything The Holy Spirit tells you now to give to Him for Jesus to be Lord of and to make certain you have not missed anything:

- _____
  _____
  _____

Then pray as follows and also give Jesus the causes and results of all these things.

General Repentance

Lord, Jesus, I want You to be Lord of all my life. I give it all to You, as well as anything that stands between You and me, whether I know they are there.

Show me these things Lord that separate us so I can deal with them as you want me to deal with them. I want to do Your Will in all I do Lord, and I ask You to help me to do this. I give it all to Jesus for Him to be Lord of so that He is Lord of all I am.

Did God show you anything?

_____
_____
_____
_____
_____

Step 2
Repent
You may need to repent of a sin you know you are doing.

What sins do you need to repent of?

_____   _____
_____   _____
_____   _____

You may need to pray:
Lord, I repent and want to stop doing anything that I am doing that is wrong. Help me to do this so you can be completely Lord of my life.

Forgive
The Lord says you are to forgive everyone who has hurt you in any way. If you deliberately do not forgive anyone who has hurt you, the Father in Heaven cannot forgive your wrongs against Him, so, you do not go to Heaven (see Matthew 6:14-15).

Who do you need to forgive?

_____   _____
_____   _____
_____   _____

You may need to pray as follows:

Jesus, I forgive all who have hurt me. Lord! Help me to forgive those I have problems forgiving. So, I can obey you in this area.

Reconcile

Give any problems you have reconciling to another (this is usually caused by unforgiveness or fear of people).

Who do you need to reconcile with?

_____   _____
_____   _____
_____   _____

You may need to pray as follows:

Lord Help me to reconcile with those I need to reconcile with and do what I need to reconcile.

Step 3
Cast Out Satan

Now, command aloud for Satan to leave and take with him all he did to you.

Satan, I have given all, these areas of my life, to Jesus to be Lord of. So, you must go from these areas in Jesus' name to the Throne of Judgment to be dealt with by Jesus. In Jesus' Name, you are to take with you everything in, on or around me or that you have done to me at any time.

Step 4
Healing and Restoration

In accordance with the Will of God, I command in Jesus' Name, healing of everything Satan did to me and in Jesus' Name, I command restoration of a sound mind, as well as all else that Satan took from me.

Step 5
Holy Spirit Infilling

Holy Spirit, please fill me completely, refresh me and anoint me freshly to serve you as an obedient citizen of the Kingdom of God, and member of The Body of believers on earth.

The following prayer gives permission to Jesus to do whatever He needs to do for you, without asking your permission and needs to be prayed only once or repeated, only if The Holy Spirit says to do so:

Father, Lord Jesus, Holy Spirit, ministering angels—I give you all permission to do anything you need to do to me, or for me, without the need to ask my permission to do these things. In the strong name of Jesus I pray, Amen.

Satan will try and convince you by placing thoughts in you or emotions on you that you have not been delivered. Just give these thoughts to Jesus using the following five steps which form the basis of the prayer above.

The Five Steps in summary:

- Give it to Jesus to be Lord of.
- Repent, forgive, reconcile.
- Cast out Satan.
- Command healing and restoration.
- Ask Holy Spirit to fill you completely.

Attacks of Satan

How does Satan attack (an overview)?

Satan can only have you do something if you let him persuade you to do it. You must accept what he offers you, before you will do what he desires you to do, rebel against God and sin.

Satan attacks you by placing thoughts in your mind, emotions and/or attitudes in your soul or feelings/sensations in your body. He also tries to have you become angry, react, reason out something or assume things without checking their factualness so he can guide you in the situation. He tries to deceive you from the truth of a situation or distract you from what Jesus wants you to do. He must persuade you to reject The Lordship of Jesus in an area so he can obtain authority over it. This is the only way he can obtain any authority over you and cause you to sin.

Use of the Five Steps to defeat Satan and his attacks.

The Five Steps are used to attack and defeat Satan and are the basis of the deliverance prayer.

The five steps are used:
- When Satan is attacking you personally or things you are steward of.
- To fight the temptations of Satan.
- To deal with weaknesses and fears in your life that lead to sin.
- To remove the damage Satan has caused to you (deliverance) as well as to restore (in accordance with the Will of Jesus), what Satan took from you.
- To protect current or future activities by stopping Satan from attacking or using them (See Steps 1, 3, and 5).
- The name of Jesus is used for spiritual warfare for others.

How to Hear the Holy Spirit

It is important to be able to hear The Holy Spirit clearly as He is your guide to live as Jesus desires you to live and to fight Satan in the way Jesus desires you to fight Satan. Remember that to be an adopted child of The Father you need to be led by The Holy Spirit (Romans 8:14).

Preparatory Prayer

Lord, I want to hear The Holy Spirit so I can do Your will and be led to be Your follower and live as Your adopted son or daughter. I give this desire to You, and I am sorry for anything I have done wrong in this area or associated areas of hearing The Holy Spirit. In Jesus' name, I command any demons that are blocking me from hearing and understanding the truths that The Father, Jesus and The Holy Spirit want me to hear and understand, to go immediately in Jesus' name, to The Throne of Judgment to be dealt with by Jesus. I ask You, Holy Spirit, to take their place. In the strong name of Jesus, I pray, Amen.

How You Hear Him

Unless The Holy Spirit or Satan appear to you, they can only talk to you in your mind. When they are communicating with you, it is as if they are your own thoughts or that you are talking to yourself. People often mistake this for a disorder as if there are two personalities in them when demons are speaking audibly in their mind. Also, when The Holy Spirit is speaking, they usually think it is their own thoughts. So, you need to know who is interacting with you.

They communicate through thoughts, dreams, daydreams, emotions, sensations, feelings etc. If it is not your thoughts, or one of the other communicating methods, then it is either The Holy Spirit or Satan placing them there. You can hold a conversation with the Holy Spirit, or the demons representing Satan and ask them questions and they will answer if appropriate. Only answers from The Holy Spirit are 100% truthful. Demons will answer in a way that furthers their purposes for you.

You will need to silence your mind. You may have trouble hearing Him (The Holy Spirit) especially if you are in a place full of distractions or in a place where Satan rules. Remember, The Holy Spirit, has a still, small (quiet) voice.

He will place an impression, picture, or thought in your mind, give you an emotion, or even speak to you in an audible voice. You will know it is from Him as it will not cause you to fear. He may speak in other ways than these, but these are the normal ways. You may feel a check in your spirit which is a 'no.' If He does not reply it is also a 'no,' so you ask Him the reason why He said 'no,' as He may tell you and you may find out more by this than by the answer you wanted.

If He gives you an answer, the He gives will line up with The Bible, and you will have peace in your heart over it. Remember, God will not contradict His Bible.

Satan will try to cause you doubt about what you are hearing then cause you to reason that it is wrong or impossible so that you believe you are not hearing correctly. Satan will also at times place fear or other wrong emotions in you to cause you to doubt God's Love, Control, Plans or Purposes for you. Satan does this to take away your trust in God and His Love for you, your Joy in Him, as well as rewards and the things He has for you. He will also try to have you misinterpret or misapply The Bible in a way that suit his purposes.

At times Satan will block you hearing the Holy Spirit, so you need to cast him out and stop him from doing this and ask the Holy Spirit again what you desired to know. If you do not hear from the Holy Spirit, ask the following:

- Are you in a place in which Satan rules so that the spiritual atmosphere is blocking The Holy Spirit?
- Are you in sin and do you need to deal with it using the Five Steps?
- Are you to ask this question of The Holy Spirit?

If you do not get an answer, it may not be the time to ask.

- It may not be the time to receive the answer.
- It may not be an appropriate question to ask.
- Jesus may not want you to have the answer, so Satan will not know what Jesus is going to do and try to stop it or replace it with his version of what you are to do.
- In Jesus' Name, did you to command the demons that are blocking you from hearing the Holy Spirit to leave you?

- Do you really want to hear the answer?
- Are you seriously listening or just going through the motions of listening?

You do not really need to know what God is doing as God will always do His best for you if you seek to know Him better and to do His Will. As long as you obey what you know He asks you to do, you will be on the path He has prepared from before creation on this path are all the things He needs you to do as well as all the promises and blessings He has given you (see Matthew 6:33, and Ephesians 2:10).

The Holy Spirit is your Companion in this life, so it is necessary to be in continual communication with Him as He helps you to navigate the traps of Satan and do the Will of God.

How does Satan Attack in more detail?

Satan can only work in two ways:

- He can deceive you in part or whole.
- He can side track you from what God desires you to do.

To draw you away from the truth He must make you believe it says something it does not or does not say something it does.

To distract you from what God desires you to do he has to deceive you into accepting his direction to go in.

Satan is known as the *father of lies* so in a sense, deception is the only way he knows to work, and it is the basis for the ways he attacks people.

So how does he attack?
Satan can only attack you in four basic ways:

- Place a voice in your mind.
- Place thoughts in your mind.
- Place emotions and feelings in your mind.
- Play on the lusts of your flesh.

His purpose is to make you believe they are your own thoughts or feelings and that you are hearing, thinking, or feeling these things. This is so he can train you to think the way he desires you to think so that you will more easily accept what he suggests.

This is why the easiest way to defeat Satan is to ignore what he suggests when you realise it is from him and not from you or The Holy Spirit. But to remove the attack you need to send the demon to Jesus to be dealt with and ask The Holy Spirit to take their place.

If Satan cannot make you then he uses gossip and character assassination to try and get you a bad reputation so people will not trust your service to Jesus believing the lies Satan has spread about you.

Remember it is war and we are told:
⁸Be on your guard and stay awake. Your enemy, the devil, is like a roaring lion, sneaking around to find someone to attack."
1 Peter 5:8 (CEV).

So, Satan is constantly looking for weaknesses in you to exploit against you. This means you need to take everything to Jesus to be Lord of in case it is Satan supplying the thought, activity, or possession.

You can see why you need to be led by The Holy Spirit in all things because something may appear to be good, but it has actually been provided by Satan to distract you into doing something that is second best when compared to what God actually desires you to do for Him.

One advantage we have is that The Holy Spirit gives us peace when something is from God and a lack of peace when it is not unless you desire something so much that your desire blots out the warning from The Holy Spirit.

So how do we deal with the attacks of Satan?

You either ignore them or send the attacking demon(s) in Jesus' Name to Jesus to be dealt with and ask the Holy Spirit to replace them. Using the Five Steps also does any deliverance needed.

You also must guard what you input into your mind and body are so that Satan cannot sneak into you through using one of these access points. Therefore, you need to ask yourself if Jesus would accept that input and if He would not then you shouldn't either.

Remember! You alone determine what goes into your soul and you alone will be to blame for what you allowed in which you knew weren't godly and had to be from Satan.

Credit: The Deliverance Handout by Neville Salvetti http://nevillesalvetti.com/

Final Thoughts

In the dictionary, freedom is defined as the power or right to act, speak, or think without hindrance or restraint. It further describes it as liberation from slavery or from the power of another. That definition completely wraps up everything Christ has done for us. There is only one thing left for you to do. Live free, unquestionably. Here's what Paul says in Galatians 5:1, *¹It was for this freedom that Christ set us free [completely liberating us]; therefore, keep standing firm and do not be subject again to a yoke of slavery [which you once removed].*

Christ died to set us free from sin and from a long list of laws and regulations. Christ came to set us free—not free to do whatever we want because that would lead us back into bondage to our selfish desires. Rather, thanks to Christ, we are now free and able to do what was impossible before—to live unselfishly. Those who appeal to their freedom so that they can have their own way or indulge their own desires are falling back into sin. But it is also wrong to put a burden of law-keeping on Christians. We must stand against those who would enslave us with rules, methods, or special conditions for being saved or growing in Christ. Enjoy your freedom today and go live the life Christ has freed you to live.

Jesus delivered me, and now I'm ***Unquestionably Free***!

Afterword

by Dr. Tiajuana Smith Pittman

NOW WHAT? So, God's pulled back the sheets of your heart's desire for visualization of what you've kept covered for years. It's true! And you know it's true because your innermost parts are reeling from reading your truth through the lenses of another's truth. How dare God publicly excavate your self-deprecating thoughts against the backdrop of an arduous journey toward freedom? How dare He mentally engage you in transformational change through another's unmasking? Yet, amid a deep apprehensiveness toward disclosure, you ponder if, through implementing behavioral changes, you too could become *Unquestionably Free*.

For many of us, biblical freedom equates to the unfolding of our business. The exposing of unprotected and yes, sometimes unconfronted emotions, and experiences. Making privy to others the scathing and undiluted thoughts of our innermost parts. It's Grace (the Personhood of Christ) pursuing you! *Who me?* Absolutely. Grace is not for the perfect; but for the broken. It's for the little girl they underestimated, the woman they tormented, and the child whose shackles they tightened. It's for you!

Although LaKesha, whose Arabic and American name means *alive,* or *she who lives* embraced the process of being processed, it began with a yes. A willingness to identify areas where there was no change. Areas where she'd made temporary housing—times of rest and reflection—a place of permanency. So, the question on the table becomes, *Do I want to be* (being, to have actual existence) *free or become* (arrive, come to a place) *free?* Let's be clear, being Unquestionably Free is not for the fainthearted because it's an assurance, a sho' nuff, if you will. In John 8:36, Jesus says, *So if the Son makes you free, then you are unquestionably free.* Contextually, Jesus' comment to religious leaders is a discussion about Abraham and the concept of a spiritual "father." When Jesus claims to be doing the will of His "father," they pipe up, laying claim to their rich ancestry through Abraham. However, Jesus replies that biological fatherhood is not more important than spiritual fatherhood. How so? Because, unlike a household servant who is not a permanent part of the family, they always guarantee biological children access to their father. And if you're not a part of the kingdom family, you can be!

His analogy reveals the difference between those who merely know about God and those who have an intimate relationship with God through Christ. So, we're clear, just like LaKesha, you too must realize being unquestionably free requires a willingness to face yourself; addressing the root of temporal losses and deficits in your life. In short, the assignment entails confronting, dismantling, and unmasking the unprofitable incubation of longing to be something other than what you are. However, scripture in Psalms 139:14 says you are *wonderfully complex!*

In today's culture, one of the most distinguishable characteristics of a Christian is one's innate capacity to endure, persevere, conquer, and overcome. The loud voice Apostle John heard in heaven according to Revelation 12:11 intensifies this truth saying, *And they overcame and conquered him because of the blood of the Lamb and because of the word of their testimony, for they did not love their life and renounce their faith even when faced with death.* Its two-fold perspective personifies the area of your life that appears in disarray physically, emotionally, spiritually, relationally, and sexually is often the very pathway God will use for our self-discovery.

God will reset the operable (free will) and cause it to become inoperable. Why? Because God does not validate greatness in comfortable but uncomfortable places. The difference between a victim's mentality and a victor's mentality is perspective. Someone once said, *most people do not have enough presence to dissolve the past.* Authentically accessing one's past requires being presently present with the Holy Spirit, who helps with our weaknesses.

No matter where you are right now, know that it's temporary. Right now, you're feeling some kind of way about being processed enroute to becoming *Unquestionably Free*. I get it! The action of unraveling our painful experiences through minimal dialogue is less intrusive than unmasking and dismantling our unspoken truths. Psalm 107:20 says, *He sent His word, and healed them, and delivered them from their destructions.* Such love that God includes in your freedom package healing and deliverance from destructive thinking, mindsets, and behaviors!

To refurbish you from the inside out, Christ packaged Himself through a relatable living sacrifice named LaKesha L. Williams. An epistle read among men whose message being *Unquestionably Free* equates to being healed without scars. I know, right! Deciding to move beyond the erected memorials of fear, shame, and guilt is one of the best investments you can make. Make the investment to straddle the strategies revealed through LaKesha's journey to being *Unquestionably Free.*

Again, the process is not for the fainthearted. It requires you to get up off your sit down and be free in your thinking—seeing you through your God-purposed uniqueness in Christ. Set your mind on those things which are above—the plentiful fruitfulness of God's word. Renounce the rapist's or molester's control over you. Forgive the offenders for their ineptitude to handle the pricelessness of your existence and remain untethered. Whether an addiction to pornography, a vicious cycle of sexual trauma, or an unfavorable medical diagnosis, it doesn't marginalize the disruption of your innocence nor compartmentalize your pain!

Resist, flee, and reset your appetites to God's desires. Align misaligned areas in your life concerning the lust of the flesh, the lust of the eyes, and the pride of life. Regardless of the method, the action remains more dangerous than the desire. Run and run again if that's what it takes to stay in alignment with your purpose. Re-evaluate your adherence to God's covenantal guidelines as it pertains to the sacredness of purity before marriage. Well, what about me, you ask? No worries! God has you covered. Whether through premarital sex or sexual trauma, once you confess your sins and accept Jesus Christ as your Lord and Savior (see Romans 10:9-10 and 1 John 1:9), you're saved—forgiven, cleansed, and redeemed!

If God through the virgin birth of His Son Jesus would come to save the world; If God can keep the bloodline and virginity of a 40-year-old woman; then, what lengths would he take to have a Damascus Road encounter with you? It's an incontrovertible truth, being *Unquestionably Free* isn't predicated upon you changing once your external circumstances change! What if victory over your inner battles were possible? What if embracing the process could change your trajectory? In 2 Corinthians 9:8, God promises *to make all grace abound toward you, that you, always having all sufficiency in all things, may have an abundance for every good work.* Would you be interested in emitting a distinctively unique fragrance other than what you're currently emitting? Don't allow the knock-off fragrance of shame and humiliation or the indiscretions of your past rob you of God's promise to *perfect and complete* a good work in you.

Proverbs 3:5-6 says, *Trust in the Lord with all your heart, and lean not on your own understanding; in all your ways acknowledge Him, and He shall direct your paths.* The mere fact you're reading this book shows that God's directing your paths and giving you an array of tools (prayers, confessions, and declarations) to show up *Unquestionably Free*.

Since His *grace is enough and His strength comes into its own in your weakness. Why not quit focusing on the handicap and begin appreciating the gift?* Like yourself, someone's waiting for you to show up free for them to glean from your transformation.

It's true! Having influence or being an influencer is most profitable when speaking from a place where you are *Unquestionably Free!*

About the Author
LaKesha L. Williams

Affectionately known as Coach Kesha, LaKesha L. Williams is a mastermind in her own right. She is a world-renowned author, acclaimed speaker, publisher, and Minister of the Gospel of Jesus Christ. As an overcomer by birth, she founded Born Overcomers Inc., a non-profit outreach ministry serving the needs of individuals and sharing the love of Christ with them. This dynamic strategic visionary and life coach is also the lead visionary of The VTF Group LLC, a top-notch publishing house that is known for multiple national and international best-sellers.

As a 16x Bestselling author and publisher, LaKesha has authored twelve solo books and she has also been a featured co-author in six anthologies, including Open Your G.I.F.T.S., presented by actress and comedian Kim Coles. Her most recent project, Grandma's Hats, just won Best Children's Book. She was also nominated by Black Authors Rock as Author of the year. This dynamo of talent and former comedian is also the creator of Hustle God's Way, a popular brand that includes clothing, planners, and journals.

As a student of Capital Bible Seminary, LaKesha is pursuing a master's degree in Christian Care. She is a board-certified master mental health coach, a certified professional Christian life coach, and a trained sexual assault victim advocate. As a virgin herself, LaKesha is an advocate of abstinence, purity, and virginity until marriage.

LaKesha lives in Maryland and enjoys serving the community. She is a member of The Remnant of Hope International Church in Prince Frederick, Maryland, under the leadership of Pastor Margo Gross. When she is not serving or working, LaKesha can be found spending time with her family and close friends, watching movies, trying new restaurants, sharing laughs, and creating new memories.

Contact Information

Phone: 301-659-2894

Email: info@coachkesha.com

Website: www.coachkesha.com

Other Books by LaKesha L. Williams

Born Overcomers

How to Overcome Negative Thinking

How to Overcome Lust

How to Overcome Rape

How to Overcome Sickness and Health Challenges

How to Overcome Discontentment

Open Your G.I.F.T.S.

Born Overcomers: A Guide to Overcoming

Triumphant Overcomers

Hope for the Overcomers Soul

Hope is Here

Restoration Speaks: Tragedy to Triumph

Pray Hustle Repeat

Study Hustle Repeat

Plan Hustle Repeat

Grandma's Hats

Life After...

Just Be You Journal

Color With Me

About the Publisher

The VTF Group LLC offers a variety of publishing options.

The VTF Group has earned its positive reputation because we go out of our way to provide truly exceptional service to each of our customers, something we like to call—"The White Glove Experience."

We believe that publishing a book is about more than becoming an author. It is about bringing a vision to fruition, building an audience, and expanding your influence.

Not all publishers are created equal, and we know that when extra attention is needed, our "White Glove Experience" will not disappoint.

As an experienced team of authors, we also specialize in coaching you through the publishing process and bringing your vision to fruition.

Contact us today to schedule a free 15-minute consultation via www.TheVTFGroup.com

Made in the USA
Middletown, DE
22 February 2023